SECOND EDITION

NEW PASSWORD 2
A READING AND VOCABULARY TEXT

Linda Butler
Holyoke Community College

PEARSON
Longman

For Jim, Miles, and Clare

New Password 2: A Reading and Vocabulary Text
Copyright © 2010 by Pearson Education, Inc.
All rights reserved.

Pearson Education, 10 Bank Street, White Plains, NY 10606

Staff credits: The people who made up the *New Password 2* team, representing editorial, production, design, and manufacturing, are: Pietro Alongi, Rhea Banker, Dave Dickey, Jaime Lieber, Maria Pia Marrella, Amy McCormick, Linda Moser, Carlos Rountree, Jennifer Stem, and Paula Van Ells.

Development editor: Thomas Ormond
Project editor: Helen B. Ambrosio
Text design & composition: ElectraGraphics, Inc.
Cover design: Maria Pia Marrella
Cover photos: Anders Ryman/Corbis and iStockphoto.com
Illustrations: Susan Tait Porcaro

Text credits, photography credits, references, and acknowledgments appear on page xii.

Library of Congress Cataloging-in-Publication Data

Butler, Linda
 New password 2 : a reading and vocabulary text / Linda Butler. — 2nd ed.
     p. cm.
 Includes index.
 Rev. ed of: Password 2, 1st. ed. 2004.
 ISBN-13: 978-0-13-246306-5 (pbk.)
 ISBN-10: 0-13-246306-7 (pbk.)
 ISBN-13: 978-0-13-246301-0 (pbk. with cd)
 ISBN-10: 0-13-246301-6 (pbk. with cd)

1. English language—Textbooks for foreign speakers. 2. Reading comprehension—Problems, exercises, etc. 3. Vocabulary—Problems, exercises, etc. I. Title. II. Title: New password two.
 PE1128.B86138 2010
 428.6'4—dc22
                                                2009020979

PEARSON LONGMAN ON THE **WEB**

Pearsonlongman.com offers online resources for teachers and students. Access our Companion Websites, our online catalog, and our local offices around the world.

Visit us at **pearsonlongman.com**.

Printed in the United States of America
ISBN-13: 978-0-13-246306-5   4 5 6 7 8 9 10—V057—15 14
ISBN-13: 978-0-13-246301-0   8 9 10—V057—15 14

CONTENTS

SCOPE AND SEQUENCE

Unit/Chapter	Developing Reading Skills	Developing Other Language Skills	Target Vocabulary
UNIT 1: Free Time			
Chapter 1: Daring to Breakdance	• Guessing word meanings from context • Identifying the topic and main idea • Interpreting a title • Identifying topics of paragraphs • Correcting a summary	• Discussion • Using new words • Writing about your free time • Word Grammar: "Myself" and other Reflexive Pronouns	*add, alone, basic, describe, each other, get interested in, myself, own, practice, respect, shy, style*
Chapter 2: In the Kitchen with Hannah	• Identifying topics of paragraphs • Sentences with *because* • Identifying the main idea	• Discussion • Using new words • Writing about things you're looking forward to • Word Grammar: Nouns	*age, become, even, give up, good at, look forward to, opinion, product, result, surprise, sweet, take, while*
Chapter 3: A Long-Distance Runner	• Scanning • Sentences with *because* • Correcting a summary	• Discussion • Using new words • Writing about feeling nervous • Word Grammar: Verbs	*about, crazy, distance, enough, exercise, give up, go on, health, mind, mountain, nervous, race, several, soft*
Chapter 4: Playing with Words	• Identifying topics of paragraphs • Scanning • Identifying the main idea	• Interview • Using new words • Writing a paragraph on your choice of topic • Word Grammar: *Another* and *The Other*	*another, education, especially, fact, favorite, look up, luck, simple, skill, spell, tiny, travel, well, worth*
UNIT 1 Wrap-up	• Review of the target vocabulary • Expanding Vocabulary: Words as nouns or verbs • Building Dictionary Skills: Using guidewords		
UNIT 2: Places			
Chapter 5: Antarctica	• Scanning • Identifying the main idea	• Discussion • Using new words • Writing a paragraph on a place you want to visit • Word Grammar: Adjectives	*above, below, continent, empty, however, land, of course, percent, scientist, shine, size, temperature, what about, would like*
Chapter 6: The Galápagos	• Understanding pronoun reference • Scanning • Correcting a summary	• Categorizing • Using new words • Writing a paragraph on your choice of topic • Word Grammar: *Else*	*beach, belong to, cool, else, government, island, north, protect, rock, second, strange, such as, unusual, west*

Unit/Chapter	Developing Reading Skills	Developing Other Language Skills	Target Vocabulary
Chapter 7: San Marino	• Scanning • Identifying the main idea	• Discussion • Categorizing • Using new words • Writing a paragraph on your city or hometown • Word Grammar: *Get* + Noun or Adjective	*ahead, capital, collect, completely, count, farm, find out, get, history, imagine, only, probably, roof, stone, whole*
Chapter 8: Mount Fuji	• Scanning • Sentences with *because* • Correcting a summary	• Sharing opinions • Using new words • Writing advice for a visitor to your country • Word Grammar: *Good, Better,* and *Best*	*actually, ago, artist, best, breathe, climb, dangerous, draw, foreign, once, paint, shape, too much, tradition, twice*
UNIT 2 Wrap-up	• Review of the target vocabulary • Expanding Vocabulary: Word families (nouns, verbs, and adjectives) • Building Dictionary Skills: Abbreviations		

UNIT 3: Our Bodies

Unit/Chapter	Developing Reading Skills	Developing Other Language Skills	Target Vocabulary
Chapter 9: Your Sense of Taste	• Identifying topics of paragraphs • Writing about topics in the reading • Organizing a summary	• Sharing opinions • Using new words • Writing a paragraph on a taste or smell • Word Grammar: *Taste*	*affect, brain, cannot stand, consider, decision, depend, matter, relationship, salty, sense, sight, still, taste, through, touch*
Chapter 10: Bones	• Scanning • Identifying topics of paragraphs • Writing about topics in the reading	• Discussion • Using new words • Writing a paragraph on eating well • Word Grammar: The Parts of Speech	*adult, bone, elbow, fix, heart, human, knee, make up, metal, middle, plastic, shoulder, support, take care of, type*
Chapter 11: Giving Blood	• Sentences with *because* • Organizing a summary	• Discussion • Using new words • Writing a paragraph on nurses' jobs • Word Grammar: *Too* vs. *Either*	*accept, accident, blood, either, emergency, lucky, match, mind, nurse, patient, reason, receive, special, store, used to*
Chapter 12: Can You Give Me a Hand?	• Scanning • Sentences with *because*	• Discussion • Using new words • Writing a paragraph using an idiom to describe someone • Word Grammar: Phrasal Verbs	*advice, already, and so on, clear, figure out, gold, idiom, instead, kind, mention, perhaps, private, secret, trust, usual*
UNIT 3 Wrap-up	• Review of the target vocabulary • Expanding Vocabulary: Prefixes (*un-*) • Building Dictionary Skills: Multiple meanings and uses of words		

Unit/Chapter	Developing Reading Skills	Developing Other Language Skills	Target Vocabulary
UNIT 4: Career Paths			
Chapter 13: Singing for Iraq	• Scanning • Organizing a summaryr	• Discussion • Using new words • Writing a paragraph about yourself growing up • Word Grammar: Verbs in the Simple Past Tense	*be born, career, celebration, dream, electricity, finally, grow up, mark, midnight, news, pretty, situation, sound, throughout, trouble*
Chapter 14: From Play to Work	• Pronoun reference Sentences with *because* • Organizing a summary	• Discussion • Using new words • Writing a paragraph on what makes a good job • Word Grammar: Word Families: *Graduation*	*along, at first, away, ever, get to, graduation, profession, program, project, proud, regular, relax, schedule, serious, variety*
Chapter 15: Listening for the Truth	• Identifying topics of paragraphs • Writing about topics in the reading • Completing a summary	• Discussion • Using new words • Writing a paragraph on a job with a lot of responsibility • Word Grammar: Word Families: *Disagreement*	*ability, among, argue, confident, court, disagreement, doubt, enter, follow, judge, law, lawyer, promise, responsibility, tell the truth*
Chapter 16: Trying to Understand	• Pronoun reference • Sentences with *because* • Organizing a summary	• Sharing opinions • Using new words • Writing a paragraph about yourself and a family member • Word Grammar: *One* and *Ones*	*chance, compare, crowd, explain, factory, fail, grade, one, prison, relative, research, smart, succeed, success, wonder*
UNIT 4 Wrap-up	• Review of the target vocabulary • Expanding Vocabulary: Suffixes • Building Dictionary Skills: Multiple meanings and uses of words; verb forms		
UNIT 5: Celebrations			
Chapter 17: Songkran	• What the reading does and doesn't say • Completing a summary	• Interviewing • Using new words • Writing a paragraph on a holiday you enjoyed as a child • Word Grammar: *Used To*	*culture, expect, extremely, fresh, had better, holiday, last, pour, put on, religion, shoot, take place, traditional, used to, wish*
Chapter 18: Québec's Winter Carnival	• Identifying topics of paragraphs • Writing about topics in the reading • Completing a statement of the main idea	• Discussion • Using new words • Writing a paragraph about the perfect meal • Word Grammar: Measure Words + Adjectives	*afterwards, be able to, couple, experience, festival, guest, narrow, order, perfect, regular, sound, thick, while, wide, would rather*

Unit/Chapter	Developing Reading Skills	Developing Other Language Skills	Target Vocabulary
Chapter 19: Celebrating a New Baby	• What the reading does and doesn't say • Sentences with *because* • Writing a summary	• Discussion • Using new words • Writing a paragraph about your life • Word Grammar: Count and Noncount Nouns	*common, cultural, dress up, event, exciting, gift, have (something) in common, plant, protection, religious, rule, so, until, wedding, wonderful*
Chapter 20: Some Unusual Celebrations	• What the reading does and doesn't say • Writing a summary	• Discussion • Using new words • Writing a paragraph on your choice of topics • Word Grammar: Quantifiers with Noncount Nouns	*be supposed to, calendar, end up, friendship, funny, invent, less, make sense, make up, pound, public, single, toe, weird, wild*
UNIT 5 Wrap-up	• Review of the target vocabulary • Expanding Vocabulary: Synonyms and antonyms • Building Dictionary Skills: Count and noncount nouns		

THE SECOND EDITION OF THE *PASSWORD* SERIES

Welcome to *New Password*, the second edition of *Password*, a series designed to help learners of English develop their reading skills and expand their vocabularies. The series offers theme-based units consisting of:

- engaging nonfiction reading passages,
- a variety of skill-development activities based on the passages, and
- exercises to help students understand, remember, and use new words.

With this new edition, the *Password* series expands from three levels to five. Each book can be used independently of the others, but when used as a series, the books will help students reach the 2,000-word vocabulary level in English, at which point, research has shown, most learners can begin to read unadapted texts.

The series is based on two central ideas. The first is that the best way for learners to develop their ability to read English is, as you might guess, to practice reading English. To spark and sustain the student's motivation to read, "second language reading instruction must find ways to avoid continually frustrating the reader."[1] Learners need satisfying reading materials at an appropriate level of difficulty, materials that do not make them feel as if they are struggling to decipher a puzzle. The level of difficulty is determined by many factors, but one key factor is the familiarity of the vocabulary. Note that

> There is now a large body of studies indicating that poor readers primarily differ from good readers in context-free word recognition, and not in deficiencies in ability to use context to form predictions.[2]

To be successful, readers must be able to recognize a great many words quickly. So in addition to providing engaging reading matter, the *New Password* series carefully controls and recycles the vocabulary.

The second idea underlying the design of the series is that textbooks should teach the vocabulary that will be most useful to learners. Corpus-based research has shown that the 2,000 highest-frequency words in English account for almost 80 percent of the running words in academic texts.[3] These are thus highly valuable words for students to learn, and these are the words targeted in the *Password* series.

The chart below shows the number of words that each *New Password* book assumes will be familiar to the learner, and the range of the high-frequency vocabulary targeted in the book.

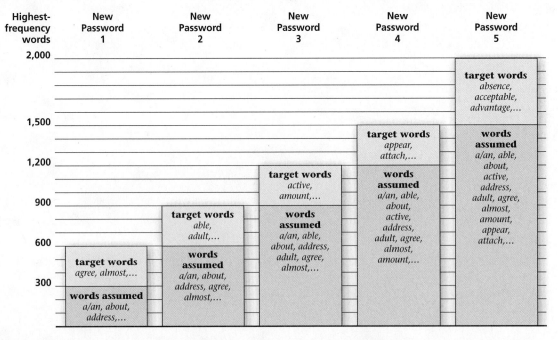

Highest-frequency words	New Password 1	New Password 2	New Password 3	New Password 4	New Password 5
2,000					target words *absence, acceptable, advantage,...*
1,500				target words *appear, attach,...*	words assumed *a/an, able, about, active, address, adult, agree, almost, amount, appear, attach,...*
1,200			target words *active, amount,...*	words assumed *a/an, able, about, active, address, adult, agree, almost, amount,...*	
900		target words *able, adult,...*	words assumed *a/an, able, about, address, adult, agree, almost,...*		
600	target words *agree, almost,...*	words assumed *a/an, about, address, agree, almost,...*			
300	words assumed *a/an, about, address,...*				

[1]Thom Hudson, *Teaching Second Language Reading* (Oxford, UK: Oxford University Press, 2007) 291.
[2]C. Juel, quoted in *Teaching and Researching Reading*, William Grabe and Fredericka Stoller (Harlow, England: Pearson Education, 2002) 73.
[3]I. S. P. Nation, *Learning Vocabulary in Another Language* (Cambridge, England: Cambridge University Press, 2001) 17.

The vocabulary taught in the *Password* series has been carefully chosen. Target word choices are based on analyses of authentic language data in various corpora, including data in the Longman Corpus Network, to determine which words are most frequently used and most likely to be needed by the learner. Also targeted are common collocations and other multiword units, such as phrasal verbs.[4] The target vocabulary is chosen most often for its usefulness across a range of subjects but occasionally for its value in dealing with the topic of one particular chapter. Other factors include the complexity of a word's meanings and uses.

While becoming a good reader in English involves much more than knowing the meanings of words, there is no doubt that vocabulary knowledge is essential. To learn new words, students need to see them repeatedly and in varied contexts. They must become skilled at guessing meaning from context but can do this successfully only when they understand the context. Research by Paul Nation and Liu Na suggests that "for successful guessing [of unknown words] . . . at least 95% of the words in the text must be familiar to the reader."[5] For that reason, the vocabulary in the readings has been carefully controlled so that unknown words should constitute no more than five percent of the text. The words used in a reading are limited to those high-frequency words that the learner is assumed to know plus the vocabulary targeted in the chapter and target words and phrases recycled from previous chapters. New vocabulary is explained and practiced in exercises and activities, encountered again in later chapters, and reviewed in the Unit Wrap-ups and Self-Tests. This emphasis on systematic vocabulary acquisition is a highlight of the *Password* series.

The second edition has expanded the series from three levels to five, increasing the number of reading passages from 76 to 104 and expanding the coverage of high-frequency vocabulary. One completely new book has joined the series, the beginning-level *New Password 1*. The other books—*New Password 2, 3, 4,* and *5*—have retained the most popular materials from the first edition of the series and added new chapters. The books vary somewhat in organization and content, to meet the diverse needs of beginning- to high-intermediate-level students, but all five feature the popular Unit Wrap-up chapters and the Vocabulary Self-Tests, and all five will help learners make steady progress in developing their reading, vocabulary, and other English language skills.

Linda Butler, creator of the Password *series*

Additional References

Nation, Paul. *Teaching and Learning Vocabulary.* New York: Newbury House, 1990.

Schmitt, Norbert, and Michael McCarthy, eds. *Vocabulary: Description, Acquisition, and Pedagogy.* Cambridge, UK: Cambridge University Press, 1997.

Schmitt, Norbert, and Cheryl Boyd Zimmerman. "Derivative Word Forms: What Do Learners Know?" *TESOL Quarterly* 36 (Summer 2002): 145–171.

---

[4]Dilin Liu, "The Most Frequently Used Spoken American English Idoims: A Corpus Analysis and Its Implications," *TESOL Quarterly* 37 (Winter 2003): 4, 671-700.
[5]Nation 254

OVERVIEW OF *NEW PASSWORD 2*

New Password 2 is intended for students with a vocabulary of about 600 words in English, and it teaches over 300 more. From twelve to fifteen words and phrases from each nonfiction reading passage are targeted in the exercises for that chapter and recycled in later chapters. Because of the systematic building of vocabulary, as well as the progression of reading skills exercises, it is best to do the chapters in order.

Most of the target words are among the 900 highest-frequency words in English, words that students need to build a solid foundation for their language learning. Other, lower-frequency words and phrases are targeted for their usefulness in discussing a particular theme, such as *career* and *profession* in Unit Four: Career Paths.

Organization of the Book

New Password 2 contains five units, each with four chapters followed by a Wrap-up section. Vocabulary Self-Tests are found after Units 2, 4, and 5. At the end of the book you will find the answers to the Self-Tests and an index to the target vocabulary.

THE UNITS   Each unit is based on a theme and includes four chapters built around readings that deal with real people, places, and events.

THE CHAPTERS   Each of the four chapters in a unit is organized as follows:

Getting Ready to Read—The chapter opens with a photo or illustration and pre-reading questions or tasks. These are often for pair or small-group work but may be best handled as a full-class activity when students need more guidance. *Getting Ready to Read* starts students thinking about the subject of the reading by drawing on what they already know, eliciting their opinions, and/or introducing relevant vocabulary.

Reading—This section contains the reading passage for the chapter. The passages progress from about 250 to about 400 words over the course of the book. Students should do the reading the first time without stopping to look up or ask about new words. You may wish to have them reread while you read aloud or play the audio, as listening while reading can aid comprehension, retention, and pronunciation. The reading is followed by *Quick Comprehension Check*, a brief true/false exercise to let students check their general understanding. It is a good idea to go over the *Quick Comprehension Check*

statements in class. When a statement is true, ask students how they know it is true; when it is false, have students correct it. By doing so, you send them back into the reading to find support for their answers. Try to avoid spending time explaining vocabulary at this point.

Exploring Vocabulary—Once students have a general understanding of the reading, it is time to focus on new words. In *Thinking about the Target Vocabulary*, students are asked to create a list of the target words and phrases from the reading. After they circle those that are new to them, they return to the reading to see what they can learn from the context of the words. They will probably benefit from working on this first as a whole class, with your guidance; later you may want them to discuss new word meanings in pairs. *Using the Target Vocabulary* follows, with three exercises of various types, to help students understand the meanings of the target words and phrases as they are used in the reading and in other contexts. These exercises can be done in class or out, by students working individually or in pairs. In *Word Grammar*, you will find exercises on parts of speech and further information about particular target words and phrases. After working through the exercises in *Exploring Vocabulary*, students can turn to their dictionaries for further information, if needed.

Developing Your Skills—In this section are tasks that require students to delve back into the reading. They include work on recognizing topics and main ideas, scanning for details, answering comprehension questions, recognizing cause and effect, determining pronoun reference, and summarizing the reading. You will also find a fluency-building exercise: *Discussion, Sharing Opinions,* or *Interviewing*. The exercise *Using New Words* has pairs of students working productively with the target vocabulary orally and/or in writing. The chapter ends with *Writing*, with students asked to write sentences or a paragraph. Sometimes there will be a choice of two or more topics related to the content of the reading. The writing exercises may be used for brief in-class writing, as prompts for journal entries, or for more formal assignments.

UNIT WRAP-UP   Each unit ends with a four-part Wrap-up section that provides a key follow-up to students' initial encounters with the unit vocabulary, to consolidate and enrich students' understanding of new words. The first part is *Reviewing Vocabulary*, with varied exercises to review word meanings; the second is *Expanding Vocabulary*, with exercises on word families, word meanings, and word parts; the third is *A Puzzle*, a crossword or word search puzzle; and the fourth is *Building Dictionary Skills*, using excerpts from the *Longman Basic Dictionary of American English* and the fourth edition of the *Longman Dictionary of American English*.

THE VOCABULARY SELF-TESTS Three multiple-choice vocabulary tests appear in the book, the first covering Units 1–2, the second Units 3–4, and the third, all five units. The answers are given at the back of the book, as these are intended for students' own use. (Unit tests can be found in the Teacher's Manual.)

The Teacher's Manual

The Teacher's Manual for *New Password 2* contains:
- The answer key for all exercises in the book
- Five unit tests with answers
- Quick Oral Reviews, sets of prompts you can use for rapid drills of vocabulary

studied in each chapter. These drills can be an important part of the spaced repetition of vocabulary—repeated exposures to newly learned words and phrases at increasing intervals—that helps students remember the vocabulary. For tips on how to use the prompts, see the Introduction in the Teacher's Manual.

To the Student

Welcome to *New Password 2*! This book will help you read better in English and teach you many new words. I hope you will have fun using it.

About the Author

Linda Butler began her English language teaching career in Italy in 1979. She currently teaches ESL part-time at Holyoke Community College in Holyoke, Massachusetts. She is the author of many ESL/EFL textbooks, including books one through four of the *New Password* series and *Fundamentals of Academic Writing*.

REFERENCES, ACKNOWLEDGMENTS AND PHOTOGRAPHY CREDITS

REFERENCES p. 12, Adapted from "Chef's Best: How Sweet It Is" by Jennifer Gabrielle. Retrieved January 22, 2009, from http://www.gazettenet. com/2008/05/23/chefs-best-how-sweet-it Used with permission of *The Daily Hampshire Gazette*.

ACKNOWLEDGMENTS First of all, I would like to thank the people who shared their stories with me so that students can enjoy them in this book: Ferdie Adoboe, Nasra Suleiman Ali, Gilberto Q. Conchas, Jad Davis, Laura Gilbert, Judith Prakash, Murat Sanal, and John Ying. I would also like to thank my students and colleagues at Holyoke Community College (Holyoke, MA, USA), whose feedback on the first edition of *Password 1* and comments on new materials were much appreciated. For research assistance, I thank Maggie Butler, Siok Kuan Lim, Naokao MacDonald, Jim Montgomery, Miles Montgomery-Butler, Thomas Ormond, and Ronnie Zhu. For her photos, I thank Clare Montgomery-Butler. I am also grateful to Lynn Bonesteel, author of *New Password 5*, for her contributions to the series.

I also very much appreciate the work of the following reviewers, who commented on early drafts of materials for the book: Simon Weedon, NOVA ICI Oita School, Japan; Joe Walther, Sookmyung Women's University, Korea; Kevin Knight, Kanda University of International Studies, Japan; Guy Elders, Turkey; Wendy Allison, Seminole Community College, Florida; Kimberly Bayer-Olthoff, Hunter College, New York; Ruth Ann Weinstein, J.E. Burke High School, Massachusetts; Vincent LoSchiavo, P.S. 163, New York; Kelly Roberts-Weibel, Edmunds Community College, Washington; Lisa Cook, Laney College, California; Thomas Leverett, Southern Illinois University, Illinois; Angela Parrino, Hunter College, New York; Adele Camus, George Mason University, Virginia.

Finally, it has been a pleasure working with Pearson Longman ELT, and for all their efforts on behalf of this book and the entire *New Password* series, I would like to thank Pietro Alongi, Editorial Director; Amy McCormick, Acquisitions Editor; Paula Van Ells, Director of Development; Thomas Ormond, Development Editor; Len Shalansky and Susan Tait Porcaro, Illustrators; Wendy Campbell and Carlos Rountree, Assistant Editors; Helen Ambrosio, Project Editor and Photo Researcher; and the rest of the Pearson Longman ELT team.

PHOTOGRAPHY CREDITS p. 1 © *Jim Cummins/ CORBIS*; p. 2 photos courtesy of Clare-Montgomery-Butler; p. 11 photos courtesy of Hannah Kaminsky; p. 19 photo courtesy of Laura Gilbert; p. 27 soccer photo reprinted with permission of *the Daily Hampshire Gazzette*. All rights reserved; p. 27 portrait courtesy of Linda Butler; p. 39, photo of Eartha by Delorme from www. RoadsideArchitecture.com © *Debra Jane Seltzer*; p. 47 © *Tropical Resources Institute, Yale School of Forestry & Environmental Studies*; p. 56 photo of Mt. Titano © *Ivonne Wierink-vanWetten/ iStock*; p. 64 © *Christie's Images/ CORBIS*; p. 79 © *Ethan Vella*; p. 80 © *Abe Rezny/The Image Works*; p. 88 © *jon challicom / Alamy*; p. 96 © *Merritt Vincent/ PhotoEdit*; p. 117 © *Tom and Dee Ann McCarthy/ CORBIS*; p. 118 © *www.ibcgroup.tv/ staracademy*; p. 126 photo courtesy Murat Sanal; p. 135 photo courtesy of Judith Prakash; p. 143 photo courtesy Marc Schultz; p. 163 © *blickwinkel/ Alamy*; p. 164 © *AFP/ CORBIS*; p. 173 © *Helmut Konrad Watson/Shutterstock*; p. 181 © *Glenda M. Powers/Shutterstock*; p. 190 © *Aaron C. Smith*

FREE TIME

Daring to Breakdance

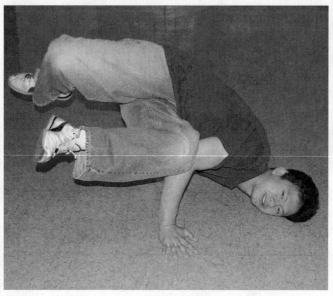

John Ying, breakdancer

GETTING READY TO READ

Talk about these questions with a partner.

1. Look at the photos of John Ying. What do they tell you about him?

2. Read the questions and write your answers. Then ask your partner.

	You	Your Partner
a. Do you like to dance?		
b. Do you like to watch people dance?		
c. Do you like to listen to music?		
d. What kinds of music or dancing do you like?		

READING

Look at the words and picture next to the reading. Then read without stopping. Don't worry about new words. Don't stop to use a dictionary. Just keep reading!

Daring to Breakdance

1   John Ying is a hard-working student at a U.S. university. He spends a lot of time sitting in class and a lot of time working at his computer. All that sitting is hard for John. He likes to be up and moving. You can see it in the way he breakdances.

2   It is not easy to **describe** breakdancing. John calls it part dance, part martial arts,¹ and part gymnastics.² He says, "First, you need to learn some **basic** moves and understand the main ideas. But then, you **add** to it. Breakdancers all have their **own** moves. You have to find your own **style**." Dancers do not always agree on what is and is not real breakdancing, John says. "But most breakdancers show **respect** for **each other**."

3   John started breakdancing when he was thirteen years old. He says, "I saw some people breakdancing, and I really liked it." He went home and looked for breakdance videos online.³ He wanted to learn to do it, but he was afraid to try. "I thought⁴ I couldn't dance because I'm hearing-impaired."⁵

4   John learned a lot from studying videos of breakdancers. "I had no one to teach me, so I had to teach **myself**," he says. "That was hard." John was **shy**, so at first, he always danced **alone**. Later, in high school, some of his friends **got interested in** breakdancing. Then they **practiced** together.

5   Today John likes practicing with other dancers at school. He is part of a breakdance group at his university. Sometimes he breakdances at parties, too. He is not shy now. He likes to show what he can do.

¹ *martial arts* = fighting sports like karate and judo

² *gymnastics*

³ *online* = using the Internet

⁴ *thought* = the simple past tense of *think*

⁵ *I'm hearing-impaired* = I can't hear as well as most people can

Quick Comprehension Check

Read these sentences about the reading. Circle T (true) or F (false).

1. John is a college student.   (T) F

2. Breakdancers do not all dance the same way.   T   F

3. John started learning to breakdance at his
   university.   T   F

4. He learned from watching videos of breakdancers. T   F

5. In the beginning, he was afraid to breakdance.   T   F

6. He doesn't like to dance with other people.   T   F

EXPLORING VOCABULARY

Thinking about the Target Vocabulary

Guessing Meaning from Context

We use words in a **context**. The context of a word means the words
and sentences before and after the word. The context can help
you guess a word's meaning. For example, look at the context of
describe:

> *It is not easy to **describe** breakdancing. John calls it part dance,
> part martial arts, and part gymnastics.*

John is describing breakdancing. He is giving information about it to
help us understand it. The context of *describe* tells you that the word
means "tell what something is like."

A Look at these words and phrases from "Daring to Breakdance" on page 3. They are the **target words and phrases** for this chapter. The list is **in alphabetical order**.

1. add
2. alone
3. basic
4. describe

5. each other
6. got interested in
7. myself
8. own

9. practiced
10. respect
11. shy
12. style

B Which words and phrases are new to you? Circle them here. Then find them in the reading. Look at the context. Can you guess the meaning?

Using the Target Vocabulary

A These sentences are **about the reading**. Complete them with the words and phrases in the box.

✔add	myself	practice	shy
each other	own	respect	styles

1. John says breakdancers need to learn some basic moves first. Then they _____add_____ something new. They put things together.
2. Each breakdancer has his or her _____ way of dancing, not like any other dancer's way.
3. Breakdancers are all different. They all have their own moves. They have different _____ of breakdancing.
4. Breakdancers often have different ideas about what real breakdancing is. But most of them show _____ for other dancers. They don't say bad things about other dancers' ideas.
5. When two people respect _____, each person thinks and says good things about the other person.
6. John didn't have anyone to help him learn to breakdance. He says, "I had to teach _____." He was his own teacher.

7. When John was young, it wasn't always easy for him to be with other people. He didn't want other people to watch him breakdancing. He was _____.

8. When you want to learn to do something well, you need to spend time working at it. You have to _____.

B These sentences use the target words and phrases **in new contexts.** Complete them with the words and phrases in the box.

add	myself	practices	shy
✔each other	own	respect	style

1. Chris and Pat love ___each other___, so they're going to get married.

2. I need to _____ more sugar to this coffee.

3. He _____ the piano for an hour every day.

4. Everyone has great _____ for her work as a doctor.

5. It's hard to get those children to talk. They're very _____.

6. I hurt _____ when I fell out of the tree.

7. Hey, that's mine! Get your _____ ice cream!

8. I read all that writer's books. I love her _____ of writing.

C Read these sentences. Match the **boldfaced** target words and phrases with their definitions.

a. She doesn't live **alone**. She lives with her sister.

b. Can you **describe** the driver of the other car?

c. When did you **get interested in** making your own clothes?

d. I don't understand baseball. Can you give me the **basic** idea of the game?

**Target Words
and Phrases**   **Definitions**

1. ___describe___ = tell what a person or thing is like or looks like

2. _____ = start to feel you want to learn more about something

3. _____ = forming the main part of something

4. _____ = not with other people

Word Grammar: *Myself* and the Other Reflexive Pronouns

John says, "I had to teach myself." He was both teacher and student.

Look at some more sentences with *I* and *myself*:

*I sometimes talk to **myself**.*

*Ow! I cut **myself**!*

The word *myself* is a **reflexive pronoun**. The reflexive pronouns are:

Singular	Plural
myself	ourselves
yourself	yourselves
himself	themselves
herself	
itself	

NOTE: *by* + a reflexive pronoun = "alone."

Example: *He lives **by himself**.*

Complete each sentence with the reflexive pronoun that goes with the boldfaced word.

1. I like to study alone. **I** like to study by _____.

2. **He** brushes his teeth and looks at _____ in the bathroom mirror.

3. They don't need help. **They** can do the job by _____.

4. **She** seems very sure of _____.

5. Are **you** teaching _____ to play the piano?

6. **We** are going to take a picture of _____.

7. A baby bird needs help. **It** cannot find food by _____.

DEVELOPING YOUR SKILLS

The Topic and the Main Idea

A Go back to page 3 and read "Daring to Breakdance" again.

B Answer the questions about the topic and the main idea of the reading.

> A reading has a **topic**. Ask, "What is the reading about?" The answer is the topic.

1. What is the topic of the reading? Check (✓) your answer.
   - ☐ **a.** How to learn to dance
   - ☐ **b.** Breakdancers
   - ☐ **c.** John Ying

> A reading has a **main idea**. Ask, "What does the reading say about the topic?" The answer is the main idea.

2. What is the main idea of the reading? Check (✓) your answer.
   - ☐ **a.** Learning to dance is fun and easy.
   - ☐ **b.** Breakdancers have to find their own style.
   - ☐ **c.** John Ying worked hard to learn to breakdance.

> The **title** of this reading is "Daring to Breakdance." Sometimes the title of a reading tells you the topic. Sometimes it tells you the main idea.

3. What does the word *daring* mean in the title "Daring to Breakdance"? Ask someone, or look it up in your dictionary. Talk with your class: Why is *daring* a good word to use in the title of this reading?

Topics of Paragraphs

**Look at the list of paragraph topics from "Daring to Breakdance."
Find the paragraph on each topic in the reading. Write the paragraph
number (1–5).**

a. John's start in breakdancing Paragraph _3_

b. how John learned to breakdance Paragraph ____

c. who John Ying is Paragraph ____

d. John's feelings about breakdancing now Paragraph ____

e. what breakdancing is Paragraph ____

Summarizing

> A **summary** tells a story again, but it is short. It has only the main
> information.

**Some of the information in this summary of the reading is wrong. Find
and correct six mistakes. The first mistake is corrected for you.**

college
John Ying is a ~~high school~~ student in the United States. In his free
time, he loves to breakdance. He started breakdancing last year. At first, he
was happy to try it because he is hearing-impaired. He learned to do it by
reading books about breakdancing and teaching himself. He was shy, so in
the beginning, he practiced with his girlfriend. Now he likes to breakdance
with friends and on TV.

Discussion

Talk about these questions in a small group or with your class.

1. How did John learn to breakdance? Tell two or more ways.
2. Why was it hard for John to learn to breakdance?
3. How did John's feelings about breakdancing change?
4. How many people in your group are interested in watching
   breakdancing or doing it?

Using New Words

These questions use some of the target words. Ask and answer the questions with a partner. Then talk about your answers with the class.

1. Who do you feel **respect** for?
2. When do you like spending time **alone**?
3. What do you need to **practice**?
4. How would you **describe** yourself?

Writing

On a piece of paper, write sentences about your free time. Answer these questions.

1. When do you have free time?
2. What do you like to do in your free time?
3. Do you usually spend your free time alone or with other people?

Example:

1. I don't have much free time during the week. I have more free time on the weekend. I usually go out on Friday and Saturday nights.

CHAPTER 2

In the Kitchen with Hannah

Hannah Kaminsky and her Lemon-Lime Sunshine Bundt cake

GETTING READY TO READ

Talk about these questions in a small group or with your class.

1. What do you see in the photos?

2. How many people in your group can cook?[1] How many can bake?[2] What kinds of food do you like to make?

   [1]You *cook* things on top of the stove.

   [2]You *bake* things in the oven.

READING

Look at the words next to the reading. Then read without stopping. Don't worry about new words. Don't stop to use a dictionary. Just keep reading!

In the Kitchen with Hannah

1   Hannah Kaminsky is a college student who spends her free time in the kitchen. She loves to cook, and she is very **good at** it. When she was eighteen, she **even** published[1] her own cookbook.

2   Hannah's cookbook has seventy-seven great recipes.[2] They are all for desserts, **sweet** foods like cakes and cookies. So it is no **surprise** to hear her say she has a sweet tooth.[3] Hannah also likes food that is nice to look at. Her cookbook has many beautiful photos of the desserts. She took all the photos herself.

3   The title of the book is *My Sweet Vegan*. A vegan is someone who does not eat animal **products**, like meat, milk, or eggs. The recipes in Hannah's book have no animal products. She **became** a vegan at **age** fourteen and started cooking for herself. For a **while**, she did not eat many sweet things. Desserts without eggs or butter were hard to find. But she did not want to **give up** desserts. That was when she got interested in baking.

4   At school, there is no kitchen for Hannah to use. So on many weekends, she goes home to bake. She thinks of new recipes and tests her ideas. It can **take** many tries to get good **results**.

5   Hannah often brings food back to her room at school. That makes the students in her dorm[4] happy. They **look forward to** trying the things she makes. Hannah says, "If you have food, you are everyone's best friend."[5] She loves getting the other students' **opinions** and ideas. Those ideas may help her write her next cookbook.

[1] *published* = had a book printed for sale

[2] a *recipe* = instructions telling how to cook or bake something

[3] *have a sweet tooth* = like foods with sugar in them

[4] a *dorm* = a dormitory, a building where college students live

[5] *best friend* = the friend you like more than any other

Quick Comprehension Check

Read these sentences about the reading. Circle T (true) or F (false).

1. Hannah is a good cook.   (T)   F

2. She has a job as a cook.   T   F

3. She is the writer of a cookbook.   T   F

4. She does not eat meat.   T   F

5. She does not eat sugar or sweet foods.   T   F

6. She is a college student and lives at school.   T   F

EXPLORING VOCABULARY

Thinking about the Target Vocabulary

 Find the words and phrases in bold in "In the Kitchen with Hannah" on page 12. Write them in the list in alphabetical order.

1. age
2. became
3.
4.
5.

6.
7.
8.
9.

10.
11.
12.
13.

B **Which words and phrases are new to you? Circle them here. Then find them in the reading. Look at the context. Can you guess the meaning?**

Using the Target Vocabulary

 A **These sentences are about the reading. Complete them with the words and phrases in the box.**

give up	look forward to	results	take
✔ good at	products	surprise	while

1. Hannah can cook, she can bake, and she can take beautiful photos. She is _____good at_____ a lot of things.

2. Hannah's cookbook is all about desserts, so we know that she likes desserts. It's not new information. It's not a _____.

3. Vegans do not eat anything made from or taken from the bodies of animals. They do not eat animal _____.

4. After becoming a vegan, Hannah did not eat many desserts for a _____. After that short time, she started baking them herself.

5. Hannah likes desserts, so she didn't want to stop eating them. She didn't want to _____ desserts.

6. When Hannah tries a new recipe, it isn't always good the first time. She usually has to try again. It can _____ many tries to get it right.

7. Hannah works in the kitchen to test new ideas. The _____ of these tests are usually good to eat.

8. Hannah's friends wait for her to come back to school. They know she'll bring good food. They _____ eating it.

B **These sentences use the target words and phrases in new contexts. Complete them with the words and phrases in the box.**

giving it up	look forward to	results	takes
good at	products	surprise	while

1. Most students _____ the end of the school year.

2. Olympic athletes are people who are _____ sports.

3. It _____ an hour to go from here to there by car.

4. Joe knows fast food is bad for him, so he is _____.

5. The main _____ of that country are sugar and bananas.

6. We'll have to wait a _____ for the next bus.

7. My doctor wants to talk to me about my test _____.

8. What a _____ to see you here!

C **Read these sentences. Match the boldfaced target words with their definitions.**

a. My grandmother got married at **age** eighteen.

b. I have no money with me, not **even** a penny.

c. Most children like **sweet** foods, like candy.

d. When did he **become** interested in computers?

e. What's your **opinion** of the movie? Did you like it or not?

Target Words	Definitions
1. ____sweet____	= with sugar in it
2. _____	= begin to be, start to change into
3. _____	= a word used to show that something is surprising
4. _____	= a person's ideas or beliefs about someone or something
5. _____	= a number telling how old a person or thing is

Word Grammar: Nouns

Nouns are words for:

people	*John, man, parents, president*
places	*airport, bank, country, New York*
things	*book, computer, flower, Toyota*
ideas	*morning, problem, surprise, time*

There is one noun in each sentence. Circle the nouns.

1. They are going by (car.)

2. The teacher isn't here.

3. Describe the building.

4. The children are sleeping.

5. Dinner is ready.

6. Let's go to the store.

7. We need more information.

8. She has her own style.

9. Your opinions are important to me.

10. He needs to show some respect.

DEVELOPING YOUR SKILLS

Topics of Paragraphs

**Look at the list of paragraph topics from "In the Kitchen with Hannah."
Find the paragraph on each topic in the reading. Write the paragraph
number (1–5).**

a. Hannah as a vegan   Paragraph __3__

b. Hannah's cookbook   Paragraph ____

c. who Hannah Kaminsky is   Paragraph ____

d. Hannah's friends at school Paragraph ____

e. testing new recipes   Paragraph ____

Understanding Sentences with *Because*

Sentences with *because* answer the question *Why*? The sentences
have two parts. The part that starts with *because* can come first or
second in the sentence.

*Hannah likes making desserts **because she has a sweet tooth**.*

***Because she has a sweet tooth,** Hannah likes making desserts.*

A **Choose the best way to complete each sentence. Write the letters.**

_c_ 1. Hannah likes making desserts

____ 2. Hannah's recipes use no
animal products

____ 3. She bakes at home

____ 4. Her friends at school look
forward to her return

____ 5. Hannah likes hearing other
students' opinions

a. because she has no kitchen at
school.

b. because she brings good food.

c. because she has a sweet
tooth.

d. because their ideas can help
her.

e. because she is a vegan.

B **Circle *would* or *wouldn't*. Complete the sentence.**

I (would / wouldn't) like to read Hannah's cookbook because _____

_____.

The Main Idea

> It is important to understand the main idea of a reading. Remember:
> The main idea is the most important information in the reading.

What is the main idea of "In the Kitchen with Hannah"? Check (✓) your answer.

☐ **1.** Hannah Kaminsky wrote a dessert cookbook when she was eighteen years old.

☐ **2.** In her free time, college student Hannah Kaminsky likes to bake, and she wrote her own cookbook.

☐ **3.** *My Sweet Vegan* is a cookbook for people who do not eat animal products but love to eat desserts.

Discussion

Talk about these questions in a small group or with your class.

1. When and why did Hannah get interested in cooking and baking?

2. What is Hannah good at? Name three things.

3. Why does Hannah bring food to school?

4. A vegetarian is a person who doesn't eat meat. A vegan eats no animal products at all. Why do you think people become vegetarians or vegans? Would you do this?

Using New Words

These questions use some of the target words and phrases. Ask and answer the questions with a partner. Then talk about your answers with the class.

1. What is a good **age** to get married?
2. What is something that is hard to **give up**?
3. What kind of **surprises** do you like?
4. What are you **good at**?

Writing

What are you looking forward to in the future? Think of five things. On a piece of paper, write five sentences with *I'm looking forward to*. You can use:

- *I'm looking forward to* (noun):   I'm looking forward to the weekend.

- *I'm looking forward to* (verb + *-ing*):   I'm looking forward to **seeing** my friends on Friday night.

CHAPTER 3

A Long-Distance Runner

Laura running in a race

GETTING READY TO READ

Talk with a partner or in a small group.

1. Look at the woman in the photo. What is she doing? How does she feel?
2. On a piece of paper, make a list of things to do for exercise.
3. What do you like to do for exercise? What kinds of exercise do you *not* like?
4. How far can you run?

READING

Look at the words and picture next to the reading. Then read without stopping. Don't worry about new words. Don't stop to use a dictionary. Just keep reading!

A Long-Distance Runner

1   A lot of people like to run in their free time. Running is good **exercise**. Doctors say that exercise is important for good **health**. They suggest[1] 30 minutes of exercise three times a week.

2   Laura Gilbert usually runs three times a week. She sometimes runs alone and sometimes with friends. But 30 minutes of running is not **enough** for her. Laura likes to run long **distances**. She says, "It takes me about 40 minutes just to warm up.[2] I start feeling good after two hours." Each year, she runs **several** marathons. A marathon is 26.2 miles long (or 42.1 kilometers). Some of Laura's **races** are even longer!

3   Every year, Laura runs in a race called *Il Passatore*. It is 101 kilometers long. That is more than 62 miles. The race begins near her home in Italy. The runners start in the city and run up into the **mountains**. They start at 3:00 P.M., and some of them run all night. The race takes Laura **about** 12 hours.

4   All year, Laura looks forward to Il Passatore, but before the race, she feels **nervous**. The race is a kind of test for her. Can she do it? During the race, her legs and feet and stomach[3] may hurt. She thinks about a nice, hot shower. She thinks about her nice, **soft** bed. A part of her **mind** says, "Stop! Go home! Why are you doing this? This is **crazy**!" But she does not **give up**. She **goes on** running. "I talk to other runners," she says, "and we help each other."

5   After 101 kilometers, Laura is happy to finish the race. Twelve hours are enough.

[1] *suggest* = say something is a good idea

[2] *warm up* = get ready to do something

[3] the *stomach*

Quick Comprehension Check

Read these sentences about the reading. Circle T (true) or F (false).

1. Laura Gilbert likes to run.   T   F

2. She always runs alone.   T   F

3. Laura thinks 30 minutes of running is long
   and hard.   T   F

4. She runs in races of 26 miles and more.   T   F

5. Before a big race, Laura feels happy.   T   F

6. To Laura, a big race feels like a kind of test.   T   F

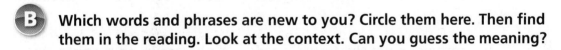

EXPLORING VOCABULARY

Thinking about the Target Vocabulary

 Find the words and phrases in bold in "A Long-Distance Runner" on page 20. Write them in the list in alphabetical order.

1. about	6.	11.
2. crazy	7.	12.
3.	8.	13.
4.	9.	14.
5.	10.	

 Which words and phrases are new to you? Circle them here. Then find them in the reading. Look at the context. Can you guess the meaning?

Using the Target Vocabulary

 These sentences are about the reading. What is the meaning of each boldfaced word or phrase? Circle a, b, or c.

1. Getting **exercise** is good for us. It's good for our bodies. *Exercise*
   means

   a. anything you do   (**b.**)moving your body   **c.** sitting quietly.
       in your free time.   to make it strong.

2. Running for 40 minutes gives Laura **enough** time to warm up. If you have enough of something, you have
   a. just a little.
   b. more than you wanted.
   c. as much as you need.

3. Laura likes to run for many miles. She likes to run long **distances**. *Distance* means
   a. how often something happens.
   b. how far it is between two places.
   c. how tall something is.

4. Laura runs in **races**. Sometimes she wins and sometimes she doesn't. A race is people doing something together to
   a. help each other.
   b. make a new product.
   c. see who is the fastest.

5. It takes Laura **about** 12 hours to finish Il Passatore. In this sentence, *about* means
   a. a little more or less than.
   b. in front of.
   c. always.

6. This race is like a test for Laura. It makes her feel **nervous**. *Nervous* means
   a. afraid or worried.
   b. good or happy.
   c. great or wonderful.

7. The race is long and difficult, but Laura doesn't **give up**. In this sentence, *give up* means
   a. stop trying to do something.
   b. work hard at something.
   c. ask questions about something.

8. Laura doesn't stop during the race. She **goes on** running. *Go on* means
   a. wait.
   b. continue.
   c. leave.

B These sentences use the target words and phrases **in new contexts.** Complete them with the words and phrases in the box.

about	enough	give up	nervous
distances	exercise	go on	race

1. Tom is going to ask the new girl to dance with him. He's feeling a little _____.

2. They can't buy a house. They don't have _____ money.

3. Jack sits and watches TV all the time. He doesn't get much

_____.

4. Some bus drivers drive long _____ every day.

5. I don't know her age, but I think she's _____ thirty.

6. Don't stop now! Please _____ and finish telling the story.

7. The Jamaican runner finished first in the _____.

8. I'll never understand this homework. I _____!

C Read these sentences. Match the **boldfaced** target words with their definitions.

a. Eat well for good **health**.

b. Do you want Chinese food tonight? I know **several** good Chinese restaurants.

c. Inez has many things to think about. She has a lot on her **mind**.

d. The Himalayas, the Andes, and the Alps are famous **mountains**.

e. Ed wants to color his hair green. I think he's **crazy**!

f. Butter is hard when it's cold and **soft** when it's warm.

Target Words	Definitions
1. _mountains_	= very high hills
2. _____	= more than two, but not many
3. _____	= easy to press into, not hard or firm
4. _____	= a person's ideas and thinking
5. _____	= how well you feel and your body works
6. _____	= surprising in a way that is foolish or bad; not using or showing good, careful thinking

Word Grammar: Verbs

Every sentence needs a **verb**. Most verbs are words for actions. For example, *run*, *fly*, *dance*, and *play* are verbs. The words *have* and *be* are also verbs.

A verb can have two parts: *is running*, *can dance*, and *don't talk*, for example. Some verbs are more than one word, like *go on* and *warm up*.

Circle the verb in each sentence. Remember: A verb can be more than one word.

1. He is on a baseball team.
2. Don't worry about it.
3. She lives alone.
4. Please describe the car.
5. He doesn't practice every day.

6. I give up!
7. It takes about two hours.
8. Don't be nervous.
9. It is becoming difficult.
10. Next, you add the sugar and the salt.

DEVELOPING YOUR SKILLS

Scanning

Sometimes you need to find a piece of information in a reading. To do this, you **scan** the reading. *Scan* means to read very quickly and look for just the information you need.

Scan the reading on page 20 for the information to complete the sentences.

1. Doctors suggest __30__ minutes of exercise __three__ times a __week__.
2. Laura says she needs about _____ minutes to warm up.
3. She says she starts to feel good after running for _____.
4. Laura runs several _____ each year.

5. A marathon is _____ long.

6. Il Passatore is _____ long.

7. The runners in Il Passatore start in _____ and run up into

_____.

8. Laura lives in _____.

Understanding Sentences with *Because*

A **Choose the best way to complete each sentence. Write the letters.**

  _c_ **1.** Doctors tell us to get exercise

  ____ **2.** Laura Gilbert runs

  ____ **3.** Il Passatore takes Laura about 12 hours

  ____ **4.** Laura feels nervous before the race

  ____ **5.** Runners sometimes talk to each other

a. because it's 101 kilometers long.

b. because it can be hard to run alone.

c. because it's good for our health.

d. because running feels good to her.

e. because it feels like a test to her.

B **Write two true sentences about yourself with *because*.**

1. _____

2. _____

Summarizing

Some of the information in this summary of the reading is wrong. Find and correct six mistakes. The first mistake is corrected for you.

long

Laura Gilbert likes to run ~~short~~ distances. She starts to feel good after

running for 2 miles. Every week, she runs a 101-kilometer race called

Il Passatore. She runs it near her home in Italy. Her legs and her feet

sometimes break during the race. The runners in this race hurt each other.

Laura always feels crazy after this race.

Discussion

Talk about these questions in a small group.

1. When and why does Laura feel nervous?

2. When do you feel nervous? Check (✓) your answers.

   I feel nervous when . . .

   ☐ I take a test in school.   ☐ I meet someone new.

   ☐ I go to the doctor.   ☐ I talk to a big group of people.

   ☐ I'm in the dentist's chair.   ☐ _____

3. Do you think long-distance runners are crazy? Why or why not?

Using New Words

Ask and answer these questions with a partner. Use one of the words or phrases in parentheses. Then talk about questions 3 and 4 with the class.

1. Are you in (good/bad) **health**?

2. How can you complete this statement? In my (book bag/bedroom/ home), I have **several** . . .

3. How much (homework/TV/exercise) is **enough** for one day?

4. How can students help **each other**?

Writing

Complete the answers to these questions. Then use your answers to write a paragraph.

• When do you feel nervous?

• What happens to you when you are nervous? Do you feel changes in your body or your mind?

• What do you do to feel better?

Example:

I feel nervous when I speak in front of the class. When I am nervous, sometimes my hands shake, and my face feels hot. I forget things to say. I look at my friends in the class, and they smile at me. They want to help me. I sit down, and then I feel better.

CHAPTER 4

Playing with Words

Ferdie at home

Ferdie at work

GETTING READY TO READ

Talk about these questions in a small group or with your class.

1. What do you see in the photos?
2. Do you ever play board games?[1]
3. How can playing games help you learn English?
4. How many of you know the game of Scrabble?

[1]Checkers, chess, and Scrabble® are *board games*.

READING

Look at the words and picture next to the reading. Then read without stopping. Don't worry about new words. Don't stop to use a dictionary. Just keep reading!

Playing with Words

1   Ferdie Adoboe's work is like some people's play. What does he do?[1] He teaches soccer and plays on a soccer team. In his free time, he plays a very different game: Scrabble, a game of words. He does it to exercise his mind.

2   Scrabble is famous around the world. You can buy the game in twenty-eight languages. The basic idea of Scrabble is **simple**. Each player gets seven letters. Players then use their letters to **spell** words and get points.[2] For example, the letters *L*, *I*, and *E* are each **worth** one point. The letter *K* is worth five. That means a player can get eight points for the word *like*. Scrabble is a game of both **luck** and **skill**. You need luck to get seven good letters. You need skill to use them **well**.

3   Ferdie says, "It's easy to learn Scrabble. You can have fun and work on your English at the same time." English is not Ferdie's first language. He is from Ghana, in West Africa, and his family speaks Fanti. But English is important in Ghana, **especially** for a good **education**.

4   Now Ferdie lives in the United States. He teaches soccer to young people all over the country. He teaches in other countries, too, so Ferdie **travels** a lot. He takes a **tiny** Scrabble game with him on the plane. He is always looking for other Scrabble players.

5   At home, Ferdie is teaching his daughters to play his **favorite** game. He also plays Scrabble online, and friends come to his house to play. Their games can take several hours.

6   Here is **another** interesting **fact** about Ferdie. He is very good at running backwards.[3] You can **look up** his name online. Ferdie set world records[4] at two distances, 100 yards[5] and 100 meters.

[1] *What does he do?* = What is his job?

[2] *points* = the numbers you win in a game

[3] *running backwards*

[4] *set world records* = did things the fastest, highest, etc., in the world

[5] a *yard* = 3 feet, or 0.91 meters

Quick Comprehension Check

Read these sentences about the reading. Circle T (true) or F (false).

1. Ferdie Adoboe is a soccer player.   **T   F**

2. Ferdie plays Scrabble in his free time.   **T   F**

3. Scrabble is a game of words.   **T   F**

4. It's a game for one person to play alone.   **T   F**

5. Ferdie is on a Scrabble team, and he teaches
   Scrabble in other countries.   **T   F**

6. Ferdie can run very fast.   **T   F**

EXPLORING VOCABULARY

Thinking about the Target Vocabulary

 Find the words and phrases in bold in "Playing with Words" on page 28. Write them in the list in alphabetical order.

1. another	6.	11.
2. education	7.	12.
3.	8.	13.
4.	9.	14.
5.	10.	

 Which words and phrases are new to you? Circle them here. Then find them in the reading. Look at the context. Can you guess the meaning?

Using the Target Vocabulary

 These sentences are **about the reading**. Complete them with the words and phrases in the box.

education	look up	skill	well
especially	luck	travels	✔worth

1. Each letter in Scrabble is _____worth_____ points. For example, a player wins five points for using the letter *K*.
2. Players hope they'll get good letters. They need _____. This means "good things that just happen" (not as the result of work).
3. Scrabble players also need _____. This means you can do something because of learning and practicing it.
4. When you have a skill, you are good at something. You can do it _____.
5. English is important in Ghana. It's _____ important in the schools.
6. Schools in Ghana use English, so people need English to get a good _____.
7. Ferdie doesn't stay at home. He _____ all over the world.
8. You can go online and _____ Ferdie's name if you want to read more about him.

B These sentences use the target words and phrases **in new contexts**. Complete them with the words in the box.

education	look up	skill	well
especially	luck	travel	worth

1. My parents don't like planes. They always _____ by car.
2. John loves ice cream, _____ chocolate ice cream.
3. Michelle became a good dancer. She learned to dance _____.

4. In the United States, "higher _____" means college or university.

5. It takes a lot of _____ to play soccer well.

6. Many people think the number 7 brings good _____ and 13 brings bad.

7. I'm going to sell my car. I'm going to ask $2,000 for it. I think it's _____ $2,000.

8. I don't know the company's address. I need to _____ the address online.

C Read each **definition** and look at the paragraph number. Look back at the reading to find the right target word. Complete the chart.

Definition	Paragraph	Target Word
1. easy to do or understand	2	simple
2. give the letters of a word in order	2	
3. very, very small	4	
4. liked more than others	5	
5. one more	6	
6. a piece of true information	6	

Word Grammar: *Another* and *The Other*

You can use *another* or *the other* + singular noun:

another book, the other book   another man, the other man

- Use *another* to mean "one more."

  *This pen won't write, so I need **another pen**.*

- Use *the other* when there are just two people or things and you mean the second one.

  *I can't find **the other shoe**.*

Complete the sentences. Use *another* or *the other*.

1. Would you like _____ cookie? We have lots of them.

2. They have two cars. One car is blue, and _____ car is red.

3. Both of my sons are in school, one boy in sixth grade and _____ boy in fourth.

4. English is just one of many languages people use in Ghana. Fanti is
_____ language they use.

5. You need a partner. Find _____ student in the class to
work with you.

6. One of her eyes is blue and _____ eye is green.

DEVELOPING YOUR SKILLS

Topics of Paragraphs

**Look at the list of paragraph topics from "Playing with Words." Find the
paragraph on each topic in the reading. Write the paragraph number
(1–6).**

    a. Ferdie and English   Paragraph __3__

    b. Ferdie's two games   Paragraph ____

    c. Ferdie's world records   Paragraph ____

    d. Scrabble at home   Paragraph ____

    e. how to play Scrabble   Paragraph ____

    f. Ferdie's work and travels   Paragraph ____

Scanning

**Scan the reading on page 28 for the information to complete the
sentences.**

1. Ferdie plays _____ in his free time.

2. You can buy the game of Scrabble in _____ languages.

3. You need both _____ and _____ to be good at
Scrabble.

4. Ferdie says you can do two things by playing Scrabble:
_____ and _____.

5. Ferdie is from _____, and his first language is _____.

6. Ferdie is teaching his _____ to play Scrabble.

7. Ferdie can _____ very fast.

8. You can look up Ferdie's name _____.

The Main Idea

What is the main idea of "Playing with Words"? Check (✓) your answer.

☐ **1.** You can play soccer and work on your English at the same time.

☐ **2.** Ferdie Adoboe loves two games: soccer and Scrabble.

☐ **3.** Scrabble is a game of words, and it's easy to learn.

Interview

Read the questions in the chart. Write your answers. Then interview a partner. Write your partner's answers.

	You	Your Partner
1. What languages do people use in your country?		
2. Is English important in your country? If you say *yes*, who uses English?		
3. Why are you learning English?		

Using New Words

Ask and answer these questions with a partner. Then talk about questions 2, 3, and 4 with the class.

1. How do you **spell** your first name?

2. What foods are **simple** to cook or make? Make a list.

3. What things are **tiny**? Make a list.

4. Brazil has good soccer teams. What's **another** country with good soccer teams?

Writing

Choose sentence 1, 2, or 3. On a piece of paper, complete the sentence and add two more sentences about the topic to make a paragraph.

1. My favorite team is _____.

2. I like to play _____, especially _____.

3. I would like to travel to _____.

Example: My favorite team is the Yomiuri Giants. They are a baseball team in my city, Tokyo. I watch them on TV, and I sometimes go to their games.

UNIT 1 Wrap-up

REVIEWING VOCABULARY

A Complete the sentences. NOTE: There are two extra words.

basic	✔each other	especially	health	product
distance	enough	even	own	while

1. Those two people love ___each other___.
2. China is big, but Russia is _____ bigger.
3. That's _____ tea for me—no more, thanks.
4. I'll be back in a _____—maybe an hour, maybe more.
5. Most students have busy lives, _____ on school days.
6. There are four dishes for the four cats. Each cat has its _____ dish.
7. Exercise and sleep are important for good _____.
8. This candy was made in Mexico. The bag says "_____ of Mexico" on it.

B Match the words and phrases with their definitions. There are two extra words.

add	get interested in	go on	look up	result
describe	give up	look forward to	respect	✔spell

1. _____spell_____ = tell the letters in a word
2. _____ = continue, keep doing something
3. _____ = put together with another thing or things

4. _____ = try to find some information (online, in a book, at the library, etc.)

5. _____ = stop trying to do something, stop working at it

6. _____ = feel happy about something that is going to happen in the future

7. _____ = tell what someone or something is like

8. _____ = start wanting to know more about something

EXPANDING VOCABULARY

Words as Nouns or Verbs

Some words can be nouns or verbs. Remember: A noun is a word for a person, place, thing, or idea. A verb is usually a word for an action.

Look at the boldfaced word in each sentence. Is it a noun or a verb? Write *noun* or *verb* on the line.

1. a. How much **sleep** do you need?   _____noun_____

   b. I **sleep** late on Sundays. Do you?   _____

2. a. Baseball **practice** is at 4:00.   _____

   b. We **practice** from 4:00 to 6:00.   _____

3. a. **Exercise** is good for your health.   _____

   b. Where do you usually **exercise**?   _____

4. a. We **respect** the other team.   _____

   b. How do you show your **respect**?   _____

5. a. We're going to **surprise** her.   _____

   b. It'll be a big **surprise**.   _____

6. a. Yoko often **travels** to other countries. _____

   b. She writes me letters about her **travels**. _____

7. a. Do you know the **results** of the game? _____

   b. The game **resulted** in a 1 to 1 tie.   _____

8. a. The boys are having a **race**.   _____

   b. Come on, I'll **race** you home!   _____

A PUZZLE

Complete the sentences with words you studied in Chapters 1–4. Write the words in the puzzle.

Across

2. Your grandmother won't tell anyone her *age* _____.
4. Good *l*_____ on your test!
7. Each singer has his or her own *s*_____.
10. Children cannot live *a*_____.
11. In my *o*_____, you need a new computer.
12. It's a *f*_____. Look it up!
13. I usually feel *s*_____ at parties.

Down

1. Mt. Everest is the highest *m*_____ in the world.
3. You go to school to get an *e*_____.
5. I'm making *m*_____ some lunch.
6. Are you *n*_____ when you fly?
7. They have *s*_____ children—four, I think.
8. The house is *w*_____ a million dollars.
9. Breakdancing takes a lot of *s*_____.

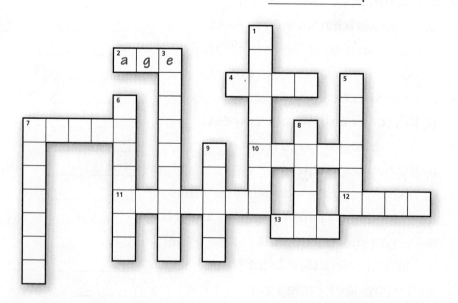

BUILDING DICTIONARY SKILLS

Guidewords help you find words in the dictionary. Look at these pages. The guidewords are *something* and *span*. *Something* is the first word on the left page. *Span* is the last word on the right page.

something	290

S

some•thing /ˈsʌmθɪŋ/ *pron*
a word you use to talk about a thing without saying exactly its name, or without saying what it is: *There is something in my eye.* | *She bought something to eat.* ➤➤ compare ANYTHING

some•time /ˈsʌmtaɪm/ *adv*
at some time in the past or the future: *I hope I'll see you again sometime.*

291	span

south•ern /ˈsʌðɚn/ *adj*
in or from the south part of an area, country etc.: *southern California* | *Do you like southern cooking?*   **S**

South Pole /ˌ. ˈ./ *n*
the South Pole the place that is the most southern point in the world, where it is very cold

A Will these words be on pages 290–291? Check (✓) *Yes* or *No*.

	Yes	No
1. somebody	☐	✓
2. so-so	☐	☐
3. somewhere	☐	☐
4. special	☐	☐
5. space	☐	☐
6. soap opera	☐	☐

B Write the words from Part A in alphabetical order.

1. _soap opera_   4. _____

2. _____   5. _____

3. _____   6. _____

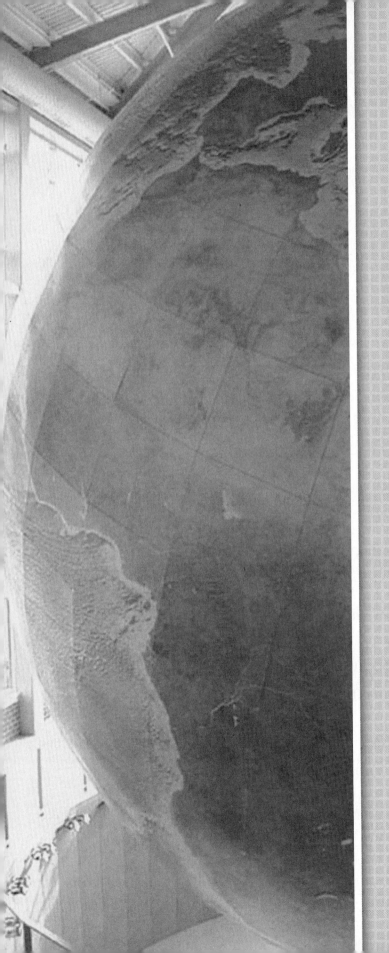

UNIT
2

PLACES
AROUND
THE WORLD

CHAPTER 5

Antarctica

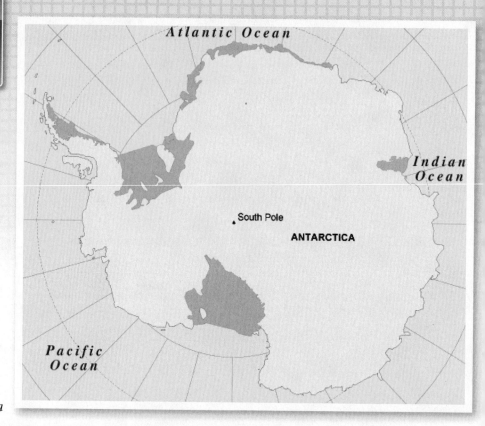

A map of Antarctica

GETTING READY TO READ

Talk about these statements with a partner. Do you think they are true or false? Circle T or F.

1. Antarctica is smaller than Australia.   T F

2. Antarctica has more than 50% of the world's fresh water.[1]   T F

3. It is summer now in Antarctica.   T F

4. There are volcanoes[2] in Antarctica.   T F

5. No one lives in Antarctica.   T F

6. Some people visit Antarctica just for fun.   T F

[1] *fresh water = water without salt, as in lakes or rivers*

[2] *a volcano*

READING

Look at the words and picture next to the reading. Then read without stopping. Don't worry about new words. Don't stop to use a dictionary. Just keep reading!

Antarctica

1   Antarctica is one of the seven **continents**.[1] Can you name the others? They are Africa, Asia, Australia, Europe, North America, and South America. All six of these continents are home to many important people, places, and things. But **what about** Antarctica?

2   Some people think Antarctica is just an **empty** place. They say, "There's nothing there—just ice and snow." But Antarctica is an important part of the world. For one thing,[2] it has almost 70 **percent** of the world's fresh water.

3   Antarctica is not the smallest continent. It is bigger than Australia, and it is bigger than Europe. It is almost the **size** of South America. There are three oceans around Antarctica. Look at the map on page 40 and read their names in English: the Atlantic, the Pacific, and the Indian Oceans.

4   **Of course**, you know this fact about Antarctica: It is *cold*. It has about 90 percent of the ice in the world. In the winter, the sun does not **shine** for several months. Then the **temperature** of the air can go **below** –110°F (–80°C).[3] In the summer, the sun shines almost all the time, but the air is never really warm. The temperature does not usually go **above** 32°F (0°C).

5   Penguins[4] live in Antarctica but not people. **However**, every year, several thousand people stay and work there. They stay for weeks or even months. Most of these people are **scientists**. They come from many different countries. They come to study changes in the weather and learn about living things in the ocean. They also study the water, the air, and the **land**. They even study volcanoes there.

(continued)

---

[1] Continents by Size

1	Asia
2	Africa
3	North America
4	South America
5	Antartica
6	Europe
7	Australia

[2] *for one thing* = here is one example or reason

[3] *–110°F (–80°C)* Say "minus . . . degrees Fahrenheit/Celsius."

[4] *a penguin*

6   A few people travel to Antarctica just for fun. They say it is a beautiful place. What do you think of that idea? Maybe you **would like** to visit Antarctica, too.

Quick Comprehension Check

A Read these sentences about the reading. Circle T (true) or F (false).

1. Antarctica is a country.   T   F

2. Most of the world's fresh water is in Antarctica.   T   F

3. Antarctica is smaller than Australia and Europe.   T   F

4. There are three oceans around Antarctica.   T   F

5. Penguins live in Antarctica.   T   F

6. People from many countries go to Antarctica to work.   T   F

B Look back at the true/false statements in **Getting Ready to Read** on page 40. Check your answers.

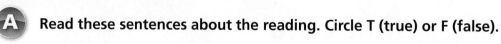

EXPLORING VOCABULARY

Thinking about the Target Vocabulary

A Find the words and phrases in **bold** in "Antarctica" on pages 41 and 42. Write them in the list in alphabetical order.

1. *above*	6.	11.
2. *below*	7.	12.
3.	8.	13.
4.	9.	14.
5.	10.	

B Which words and phrases are new to you? Circle them here. Then find them in the reading. Look at the context. Can you guess the meaning?

Using the Target Vocabulary

 A These sentences are **about the reading**. Complete them with the words and phrases in the box.

above	however	percent	what about
below	of course	shines	would like

1. Six of the continents are home to important people, places, and things. But _____ Antarctica? Is the same thing true for Antarctica, too?
2. Most of the world's fresh water—almost 70 _____ (or 70%)—is in Antarctica.
3. It's cold in Antarctica. Everybody knows that, so _____ you know that.
4. In Antarctica, the sun _____ for weeks in the summer. It doesn't go down at night.
5. The temperature sometimes goes _____ –80°C. That means it gets colder than minus eighty degrees Celsius.
6. The temperature doesn't usually go _____ 32°F. That means it doesn't usually go any higher than that.
7. People don't live in Antarctica. _____, scientists stay there for weeks or even months.
8. You may want to visit Antarctica. Maybe you _____ to travel there.

B These sentences use the target words and phrases **in new contexts**. Complete them with the words in the box.

above	however	percent	what about
below	of course	shine	would like

1. I _____ a cup of coffee, please.
2. Almost 50 _____ of the students are over twenty-five years old.

3. It's great that she's giving up smoking, but _____ her husband? Is he?

4. I don't like cold weather. _____, I love snow. It's beautiful!

5. Can you spell *cat*? Yes, _____ I can! It's simple: c-a-t.

6. At night, lights _____ from the windows of people's homes.

7. After so much rain, in some places, the water is up _____ the first floor of the houses!

8. Our apartment is on the third floor. They live _____ us on the second floor.

C **Read these sentences. Match the boldfaced target words with their definitions.**

a. Asia is the largest **continent**.

b. What **size** shoe does he wear?

c. Dr. Smith is a **scientist**. He studies the oceans.

d. She has nothing to drink. Her glass is **empty**.

e. Penguins spend a lot of time in the water, but they live on **land**.

f. It is sunny today, but the **temperature** is below 0°C.

Target Words   **Definitions**

1. _____ = holding nothing inside

2. _____ = how hot or cold something is

3. _____ = how big or small something is

4. _____ = the part of the world that is not under water

5. _____ = one of seven large areas of land in the world

6. _____ = a person who studies how things in nature are made and what they do

Word Grammar: Adjectives

> An **adjective** is a word that describes:
>
> a person: a *shy* boy, *fast* runners
>
> a place: *beautiful* cities, a *large* airport
>
> a thing: a *tall* building, *small* cars
>
> an idea: *new* information, a *nice* surprise
>
> You can use:
>
> Adjective + noun: *I have **good friends**.*
>
> The verb *be* + adjective: *Mary and John **are happy**.*

Circle the adjective in each sentence.

1. It's not (difficult.)
2. She likes sweet foods.
3. Don't be nervous.
4. This bed is very soft.
5. The glass is empty.
6. It's a simple game.
7. What a crazy idea!
8. I need some basic information.

DEVELOPING YOUR SKILLS

Scanning

Read these questions about "Antarctica." Scan the reading, and write short answers.

1. What is Antarctica? _a continent_____
2. What are the other six continents? _____
   _____
3. How much of the world's fresh water is in Antarctica? _____ percent
4. How much of the ice in the world is in Antarctica? _____ percent
5. What happens to the air temperature in the winter? _____
   _____
6. How many people work in Antarctica? _____
7. What do they study? _____

The Main Idea

What is the main idea of "Antarctica"? Check (✓) your answer.

☐ **1.** Antarctica has most of the world's fresh water.

☐ **2.** Everyone should visit Antarctica.

☐ **3.** Antarctica is an interesting and important continent.

Discussion

Talk about these questions in a small group.

1. What facts about Antarctica can you remember from the reading?

2. In the future, ships might pull large pieces of ice from Antarctica across the ocean. They would take the ice to countries that need fresh water. What do you think of this idea? Which countries might want to do this?

3. Some people visit Antarctica just for fun. Would you like to go there? Tell why or why not.

Using New Words

Work alone or with a partner. Choose five target words or phrases from the list on page 42. On a piece of paper, use each word or phrase in a sentence.

Writing

Where in the world do you want to go? Choose a place to visit and write a paragraph about it. Give three or more facts about the place. Answer these questions.

• Where is it?

• What can you see and do there?

• What's the weather like?

• Why do you want to go there?

You can begin: *I would like to visit* _____ .

The Galápagos

A map of the Galápagos Islands

A woman and a tortoise on the beach in the Galápagos

GETTING READY TO READ

Talk with a partner or in a small group.

1. Can you label the pictures of these animals? Write *a penguin, an iguan*a, or *a sea lion* under each picture.

a. _____   b. _____   c. _____

2. Name some good places to see interesting animals.

READING

Look at the words and pictures next to the reading. Then read without stopping.

The Galápagos

1   There is an **unusual** group of **islands** in the Pacific Ocean about 600 miles to the **west**[1] of South America. They are near the equator.[2] These islands are part of Ecuador, a small country in South America. In English, they are called the Galápagos.

2   The Galápagos are famous because of their animals. These animals are unusual in two ways. First, some of them live in just this one part of the world. You cannot find them anywhere **else**. For example, there are some very big tortoises here. (*Galápago* is one Spanish word for *tortoise*.) **Second**, the animals are not afraid of people. Visitors can sit down next to iguanas on the **rocks**. They can walk very close to sea lions on the **beach**. They can even swim with them in the ocean!

[2] the *equator*

3   Are you interested in birds? There are more than eighty different kinds of them here, even one kind of penguin. Penguins usually live in cold places, so finding them near the equator seems **strange**. However, cold water travels **north** from Antarctica. It brings down the water temperature around the Galápagos. It makes the water **cool** enough for penguins.

4   There are a lot of very small islands in the Galápagos. Thirteen of the islands are larger. People live on five of these, but most of the land is just for animals. Some of these animals, **such as** the tortoises, **belong to** endangered species.[3] In the Galápagos, no one will hurt them. The people of Ecuador want to **protect** these animals. Their **government** will go on working to keep the animals safe.

[3] *endangered species* = kinds of animals that soon might all be dead

Quick Comprehension Check

Read these sentences about the reading. Circle T (true) or F (false).

1. The Galápagos are a group of islands.   T   F
2. These islands are part of Ecuador.   T   F
3. They are famous because of their beautiful beaches.   T   F
4. Some unusual animals live in the Galápagos.   T   F
5. People cannot go near the animals.   T   F
6. People do not live on most of the islands; just
   animals do.   T   F

EXPLORING VOCABULARY

Thinking about the Target Vocabulary

 Find the words and phrases in bold in "The Galápagos" on page 48. Write them in the list in alphabetical order.

1. beach	6.	11.
2. belong to	7.	12.
3.	8.	13.
4.	9.	14.
5.	10.	

 Which words and phrases are new to you? Circle them here. Then find them in the reading. Look at the context. Can you guess the meaning?

Using the Target Vocabulary

 A **Label these pictures. Write** *beach*, *cool*, *island*, **or** *rock*.

1. an iguana on a _____

2. a sea lion on a _____

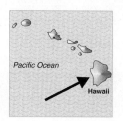

3. _____

4. an _____

 B **These sentences are about the reading. Complete them with the words and phrases in the box.**

belong to	government	protect	strange	unusual
else	north	second	such as	west

1. The Galápagos are an _____ group of islands. They are different from most other islands.

2. The Pacific Ocean is to the _____ of South America. The Atlantic Ocean is to the east.

3. The tortoises of the Galápagos live in just this one place. They don't live anywhere _____.

4. The animals are unusual in two ways. First, they don't live anywhere else. _____, they are not afraid of people.

5. It is surprising to find penguins near the equator, where the weather is usually hot. It seems _____ to find penguins there.

6. Cold water from Antarctica travels _____ and comes to the Galápagos.

7. Several kinds of animals, _____ the tortoise, live here. (The tortoise is an example.)

8. The tortoises on the Galápagos _____ an endangered species. They are part of the same species (animals of the same kind).

9. The people of Ecuador want to keep these animals safe. They want to _____ them.

10. The people who work for a country and decide things for the country are the _____. In Ecuador, they are working to protect the animals of the Galápagos.

C These sentences use the target words and phrases **in new contexts.** Complete them with the words and phrases in the box.

belong to	government	protect	strange	unusual
else	north	second	such as	west

1. About 200 countries _____ the United Nations.

2. Elephants live in Africa and India. Do they live anywhere _____?

3. I can't go with you because, first, I don't have the time, and _____, I don't have the money.

4. Workers sometimes wear safety glasses to _____ their eyes.

5. Who is the head of the _____ in your country? Is there a president? Is there a king or queen, or a prime minister?

6. Some colors, _____ light blue or green, are called "cool colors."

7. Colombia is in South America, and Canada is in _____ America.

8. Kenya and Senegal are in Africa. Kenya is in the east, and Senegal is in the _____.

9. "_____" means different from most others. Use it to describe something interesting, something you don't often see.

10. "_____" means unusual but in a way that is hard to understand and may not be good.

Word Grammar: *Else*

> The phrase *anywhere else* is used in the reading on page 41. *Else* means "different" or "other." *Else* is often used with words like *anybody*, *something*, and *everyone*.

A **Read the sentences below. Underline the word before *else*.**

1. Our teacher won't be here tomorrow. <u>Someone</u> else will teach our class.
2. I'm going to get some tea. Would anyone else like some?
3. The little boy wants ice cream. Nothing else will make him happy.
4. What should we get her for her birthday, some flowers? I can't think of anything else.
5. That part of the library is closed, but you can go everywhere else in the building.
6. This store doesn't have good clothes. Let's go somewhere else.

B **Complete these phrases. Use the words from Part A.**

1. ____someone____ + *else* = some other person
2. _____ + *else* = any other person
3. _____ + *else* = no other thing
4. _____ + *else* = any other thing
5. _____ + *else* = every other place
6. _____ + *else* = some other place

C **Complete these sentences. Use the phrases with *else* from Part B.**

1. I know Marta, but I don't know ____anyone else____ in that class.
2. He's crazy about cars. He talks about cars all the time. He talks about _____!
3. She doesn't live at her parents' house now. She lives _____.
4. We have to clean our apartment. The kitchen is OK, but we have to clean _____.
5. I'm going to the store for some bread. Do we need _____?
6. I'm sorry, but I don't know the time. Ask _____.

DEVELOPING YOUR SKILLS

Pronoun Reference

> A **pronoun** (such as *he*, *she*, *it*, or *them*) takes the place of a noun.
> We often use a pronoun so that a noun is not repeated.
>
> They
>
> *The tortoises live in just this one place. ~~The tortoises~~ don't live*
> *anywhere else.*

What do the boldfaced pronouns mean in these sentences? Look back at the reading. Write the answers.

1. Paragraph 1: In English, **they** are called the Galápagos. <u>these islands</u>
2. Paragraph 2: You cannot find **them** anywhere else. _____
3. Paragraph 2: **They** can walk very close to sea lions. _____
4. Paragraph 3: **It** makes the water cool enough for penguins. _____
   _____
5. Paragraph 4: In the Galápagos, no one will hurt **them**. _____
   _____

Scanning

Scan the reading on page 48 for the information to complete the sentences.

1. The Galápagos are about _____ miles west of South America.
   That's about 966 kilometers.
2. These islands are part of _____, a small South American
   country.
3. *Galápago* is a _____ word for *tortoise*.
4. There are more than eighty different kinds of _____ in the
   Galápagos.
5. _____ need cool water.
6. People live on _____ of the _____ larger islands in the Galápagos.
7. The _____ of Ecuador is working to protect the
   endangered species.

Summarizing

Some of the information in this summary of the reading is wrong. Find and correct six mistakes. The first mistake is corrected for you.

west

The Galápagos are islands to the ~~east~~ of South America. They are near the equator, but the ocean water is hot. The Galápagos are famous because of their beaches. The animals are not afraid of each other. Some of these animals, not the tortoises, belong to endangered species. The Ecuadorian government is working to kill them.

Categorizing

> A **category** is a group of people or things of the same kind. The people or things in a category are like each other in some way.

A **Work with a partner. Name each of these categories.**

1. Ecuador, Korea, Canada, Turkey, Russia _____countries_____

2. red, green, blue, black, yellow _____

3. Antarctica, Asia, South America, Europe, Africa _____

4. coffee, tea, juice, water, milk _____

5. soccer, swimming, tennis, basketball, baseball _____

6. parents, students, scientists, visitors, doctors _____

7. tortoises, penguins, sea lions, iguanas _____

B **With your partner, think of another category. List five people or things that belong in that category.**

Category: _____

_____

Using New Words

Ask and answer these questions with a partner. Talk about your answers with the class.

1. Can you name three **islands**? Tell where they are.
2. What country is to the **north** of us? What country is to the **west**?
3. Does your country **belong to** the United Nations?
4. What is the **temperature** today?

Writing

Choose sentence 1, 2, or 3. On a piece of paper, complete the sentence and add two or more sentences about the topic to make a paragraph.

1. I (would like / wouldn't like) to visit the Galápagos because . . .
2. A good beach . . .
3. A _____ is a good pet because . . .
   (kind of animal)

Example:

A good beach has nice, white sand. The water is clean and not very cold. There are big waves, but you can swim. There are not a lot of . . .

San Marino

A tiny country

Mount Titano in San Marino

GETTING READY TO READ

Talk about these questions with a partner or in a small group.

1. What continent is San Marino on?

2. What do you think comes from San Marino? Why?

a. grapes or bananas?

b. diamonds or building stones?

c. ships  or stamps?

56

READING

Look at the words and pictures next to the reading. Then read without stopping.

San Marino

1   Close your eyes and **imagine** this: You are a visitor to the Republic of San Marino. It is a beautiful, warm day in May. This afternoon, you have some free time. Would you like to take a walk? In one afternoon, a person can walk across the **whole** country!

2   San Marino is very small. From east to west, it is no more than 6 miles (9 kilometers) across. It is smaller than many cities.

3   Begin your walk at the border[1] between San Marino and Italy. (Italy is the **only** country that borders San Marino. San Marino is **completely** inside it.) You can see **farms** on much of the land around you. Some of San Marino's farm products are wheat,[2] olives,[3] and grapes. **Ahead** of you, in the center of the country, you can see a mountain. That is Mount Titano. Walk up the mountain to the **capital**, also called San Marino. It is one of just nine towns in the whole country. In all these towns, you will see old **stone** buildings with red **roofs**.

4   All around you, you will hear people speaking Italian. You will **probably** hear other languages, too—maybe Spanish, German, Chinese, or Japanese. You are not the only visitor to San Marino today. This little country has only 30,000 people but more than 3,000,000[4] visitors each year. No one really knows the number. The government does not stop visitors at the border to **count** them. People come and go freely here.

5   Some visitors come because they are interested in **history**. The Republic of San Marino is more than 1,700 years old. Visitors may come to see the old buildings and **find out** about the past. Others come to buy coins[5] and stamps. People all over the world **collect** the beautiful and unusual stamps of San Marino.

(continued)

[1] *border* = the line between two countries

[2] *wheat*

[3] *olives*

[4] *30,000 . . . 3,000,000* = 30 thousand . . . 3 million

[5] *coins*

6   Are you **getting** tired from your walk? Then it is time to sit down and have a nice, cool drink or a *gelato*—an Italian ice cream. Enjoy!

Quick Comprehension Check

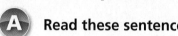 Read these sentences about the reading. Circle T (true) or F (false).

1. San Marino is a city in Italy.   T   F

2. From east to west, San Marino is just a few miles or kilometers across.   T   F

3. Bananas are an important farm product in this country.   T   F

4. Many visitors come to San Marino.   T   F

5. The government stops all visitors coming into the country.   T   F

6. Visitors can buy beautiful and unusual stamps and coins.   T   F

 Look back at the questions in **Getting Ready to Read** on page 56. Check your answers.

EXPLORING VOCABULARY

Thinking about the Target Vocabulary

 Find the words and phrases in **bold** in "San Marino" on page 57. Write them in the list in alphabetical order.

1. ahead	6.	11.
2. capital	7.	12.
3.	8.	13.
4.	9.	14.
5.	10.	15.

B Which words and phrases are new to you? Circle them here. Then find them in the reading. Look at the context. Can you guess the meaning?

Using the Target Vocabulary

A These sentences are **about the reading**. What is the meaning of each **boldfaced** word or phrase? Circle a, b, or c.

1. You aren't really in San Marino, but you can **imagine** that you are there. *Imagine* means

   a. make a picture in your mind. **b.** remember. **c.** decide or choose.

2. People can walk across **the whole** country of San Marino. The whole something is

   a. a little of it. **b.** half of it. **c.** all of it.

3. There is **only** one country that borders San Marino. *Only* means

   a. sometimes. **b.** especially. **c.** just.

4. San Marino is **completely** inside Italy. *Completely* means

   a. maybe, perhaps. **b.** all, totally. **c.** of course.

5. When you start walking across San Marino, you can see a mountain **ahead** of you. *Ahead* means

   a. in front. **b.** below. **c.** inside.

6. Many buildings in San Marino are made of **stone**. *Stone* means

   a. rock. **b.** ice. **c.** snow.

7. From a plane, you can see the red **roofs** of San Marino. *Roof* means

   a. the front of a building. **b.** the top part of a building. **c.** the inside of a building.

8. Some visitors come to **find out** about San Marino's past. *Find out* means

   a. teach. **b.** describe. **c.** learn.

9. Are you **getting** tired of walking? In this sentence, *getting* means

   a. taking. **b.** becoming. **c.** buying.

B These sentences use the target words and phrases **in new contexts**. Complete them with the words and phrases in the box.

ahead	find out	imagine	roof	whole
completely	getting	only	stone	

1. He's not like his brother in any way. The two of them are
   _____ different.

2. Do you like to listen to the rain on the _____?

3. The Kenyan runner is in first place. No one is _____ of
   her.

4. Close your eyes and _____ that you're lying on a
   beautiful beach right now.

5. Can you really eat that _____ pizza? I don't believe it!

6. Do you know who won the game? Let's look online and
   _____.

7. In the park, there are gardens with _____ walls all around
   them.

8. The ticket costs $8.00, but I have _____ $7.25.

9. I don't feel good. I think I'm _____ sick.

C Read these sentences. Match the **boldfaced** target words with their
definitions.

a. She can **count** to ten in three languages.

b. Let's give them a book about **history**. They'll like that. They **collect**
   history books.

c. I don't know why he isn't in school, but he's **probably** sick.

d. They have cows, horses, and chickens on their **farm**.

e. The **capital** of the Republic of San Marino is also called San Marino.

Target Words	Definitions
1. _____	= a piece of land where people grow food and keep animals
2. _____	= find or say how many things are in a group (1, 2, 3, . . .)
3. _____	= the city where the main government of a state or country is
4. _____	= bring things together and keep them as a group
5. _____	= likely to happen but not 100 percent sure of happening
6. _____	= the record of things that happened in the past

Word Grammar: *Get* + Noun or Adjective

> The verb *get* has many meanings. After *get*, you will often see a noun (*Get a job*!) or an adjective (*Are you getting tired*?). The words after *get* change its meaning.

 Read these sentences with *get*. In three sentences, *get* means "become." Check (✓) the sentences.

	Get = Become
1. Bob's **getting** some bread at the store.	
2. Your hair is **getting** long.	
3. He needs to **get** a new car.	
4. Don't **get** angry!	
5. It **gets** dark early in the winter.	
6. Where can I **get** a bus to the airport?	

 Circle the words after *get* in sentences 2, 4, and 5 in Part A. What part of speech are they?

C **Complete this statement:**

In sentences with *get* + _____ , the verb *get* means "become."

D **Write sentences. Use *get* meaning "become."**

1. I sometimes get hungry in class. _____

2. _____

3. _____

4. _____

DEVELOPING YOUR SKILLS

Scanning

Read these questions about "San Marino." Scan the reading, and write short answers.

1. How big is San Marino from east to west? _____

2. What country is all around San Marino? _____

3. What are some farm products from San Marino? _____

4. What can you see in the center of the country? _____

5. How many people visit the country each year? _____

6. Why do people visit San Marino? Give two reasons:

    a. _____

    b. _____

The Main Idea

What is the main idea of "San Marino"? Check (✓) your answer.

☐ **1.** San Marino is a tiny country, but it's an interesting place to visit.

☐ **2.** Small countries sell their products to people from other countries.

☐ **3.** It is easy to walk across San Marino.

Discussion

Talk in a small group or with the whole class.

1. What is unusual about San Marino?

2. Visitors to a place sometimes buy souvenirs. A souvenir helps a traveler to remember a visit. What about you? Do you have any souvenirs from your travels?

3. The words below come from the reading about San Marino. Put them into four categories. Give each category a name.

   coins, farms, gelato, grapes, Italian, Japanese, Mount Titano, olives, red roofs, Spanish, stamps, wheat

a. Languages	b.	c.	d.

_____ _____ _____ _____

_____ _____ _____ _____

_____ _____ _____ _____

Using New Words

These questions use some of the target words and phrases. Ask and answer the questions with a partner. Then talk about your answers with the class.

1. What is the **capital** of your country?

2. Do you **collect** anything? Would you like to collect something in the future?

3. Would you like to live on a **farm**? Why or why not?

4. Do you like books about **history**? Can you name any historical movies?

5. When you want to **find out** something about a person, how do you do it?

Writing

Write a paragraph about your city or hometown. You can begin: *I am from* _____. Tell where your city or hometown is. Answer these questions:

- How big is it, or how many people live there?
- What is the weather like?
- Is it famous for one or more products?
- What do you like about your city or hometown?

CHAPTER 8

Mount Fuji

*Evening Snow,
Mt. Fuji* by
Toyokuni II

GETTING READY TO READ

Talk about these questions with your class.

1. How many people in the class know the name "Fuji"? Where is Mount Fuji?

2. Mount Fuji is a volcano. What kind of volcano do you think it is? Circle your answer.

   a. an **active** volcano (Sometimes it erupts. It sends out hot rock and lots of smoke.)

   b. a **dormant** volcano (It is quiet now, but it might erupt in the future.)

   c. an **extinct** volcano (It cannot erupt any more.)

3. How many people in the class like to climb mountains?

READING

Look at the words and pictures next to the reading. Then read without stopping.

Mount Fuji

1   There is a very famous mountain in Japan. It is called Mount Fuji (or *Fuji-san*). People can see it from many parts of the country. It is more than 12,000 feet (3,776 meters) high, higher than any other mountain in Japan. It is wonderful to look at. Many people take photos of it. **Artists** often **draw** or **paint** pictures of it. They love the mountain's beautiful and unusual **shape**. The mountain is symmetrical.[1]

2   Mount Fuji is **actually** a volcano. People often forget that fact because the last eruption[2] was a long time **ago**, in 1708. Now Mount Fuji is dormant ("sleeping"), so people can **climb** to the top of it. More than 200,000 people climb it each year. Most of them are Japanese. However, a large number—about 30 percent of the climbers—come from **foreign** countries.

3   July and August are the **best** months to climb Mount Fuji. At other times of the year, it can be **dangerous**. There is **too much** snow and bad weather. Even in the summer, the climb is not easy. The air is thin on the mountain, so it is hard to **breathe**. The sun is strong, and the days can be very hot. Then at night, it gets cold.

4   Many climbers start up the mountain late in the day. They carry flashlights,[3] and they climb for hours in the dark. They want to arrive at the top before sunrise. Then they can watch the sun come up. It is becoming a Japanese **tradition**.

5   Many Japanese want to climb Mount Fuji **once** in their lives. Most of them want to climb it only once. There is a saying[4] in Japan: "A person who never climbs Mount Fuji is a fool,[5] and a person who climbs it **twice** is twice the fool."

[1] *symmetrical* = with both halves exactly the same size and shape

[2] an *eruption* = the action of a volcano sending out hot rock

[3] a *flashlight*

[4] a *saying* = a famous statement that many people think is true

[5] a *fool* = a person who does stupid or crazy things

Quick Comprehension Check

Read these sentences about the reading. Circle T (true) or F (false).

1. Mount Fuji is in Japan.   T   F

2. Many people think Mount Fuji is beautiful.   T   F

3. No one can climb this mountain.   T   F

4. It never gets cold on Mount Fuji.   T   F

5. Some people go to the mountaintop and watch
   the sun come up.   T   F

6. Most climbers drive up Mount Fuji.   T   F

EXPLORING VOCABULARY

Thinking about the Target Vocabulary

A Find the words and phrases in **bold** in "Mount Fuji" on page 65. Write them in the list in alphabetical order.

1. actually   6.   11.

2. ago   7.   12.

3.   8.   13.

4.   9.   14.

5.   10.   15.

B Which words and phrases are new to you? Circle them here. Then find them in the reading. Look at the context. Can you guess the meaning?

Using the Target Vocabulary

A Complete these sentences. Write *breathing hard*, *climbing a mountain*, *drawing a map*, or *doing something dangerous*.

1. He's _____ .

2. He's _____ .

3. She's _____ .

4. She's _____ .

B These sentences are **about the reading**. Complete them with the words and phrases in the box.

| actually | artists | foreign | painted | too much | twice |
| ago | best | once | shape | traditions | |

1. Some people draw pictures of Mount Fuji. These people are

_____ .

2. A Japanese artist _____ the picture on page 64.

3. Mount Fuji has an unusual _____ . It's symmetrical. Most mountains are not. They look different on each side.

4. Some people think Mount Fuji is all rock inside, but it's really not. Mount Fuji is _____ a volcano.

5. The last eruption of this volcano was a long time _____ (in the past). It was in 1708.

6. Most climbers on Mount Fuji are Japanese, but some climbers are from _____ countries.

7. July and August are the _____ months to climb Mount Fuji. The other months are not as good.

8. In winter, most people cannot climb Mount Fuji. There is
_____ snow and bad weather for them.

9. Sometimes the people of a country do the same thing again and
again, year after year. For example, they do the same things every
New Year's Day. These things are _____.

10. Some people climb Mount Fuji only _____ (one time).

11. Others climb it _____ (two times).

C These sentences use the target words and phrases **in new contexts.**
Complete them with the words and phrases in the box.

actually	artist	foreign	paint	too much	twice
ago	best	once	shapes	tradition	

1. It's dangerous to go there. There is _____ ice and too
many falling rocks.

2. Paola collects stamps and coins from _____ countries.

3. Doug draws pictures for children's books. He's a very good
_____.

4. This kind of fruit doesn't look good to eat, but it _____
tastes great.

5. Some Chinese people wear red clothes for the New Year. It's a Chinese
_____.

6. An orange doesn't look like a lemon. They are different colors and
have different _____.

7. Jessica says, "Toyota makes good cars. Saab makes better ones.
Mercedes makes the _____ cars of all."

8. The baby arrived about eleven months _____. He's almost
one year old.

9. We can take the test only _____. We get only one try.

10. Indira calls her parents _____ a week, on Wednesday and
on Sunday.

11. I'm going to _____ my room blue and white.

Word Grammar: *Good, Better,* and *Best*

> *Better* and *best* are related to the adjective *good*.
> - *Better* is the comparative form of *good*. Use *better* when you compare two things.
>   > *That beach is* **good**, *but this beach is* **better**.
>   > *This beach is* **better than** *that beach*.
> - *Best* is the superlative form of *good*. Use *the best* for the person or thing that is better than all others.
>   > *I think Playa Flamenco is* **the best** *beach in the whole world*.

Write *good*, *better*, or *best*.

1. Your photo is _____ than my photo.
2. Look at these six photos. Which is the _____ photo of all?
3. I think this photo is especially _____.
4. They are _____ dancers.
5. They are much _____ dancers than we are.
6. They are the _____ dancers in the group.

DEVELOPING YOUR SKILLS

Scanning

Scan the reading on page 65 for the information to complete the sentences.

1. Mount Fuji has an unusual shape for a mountain. It is

   _____.

2. People may forget that Mount Fuji is actually a _____.
3. The last eruption of Mount Fuji was in the year _____.
4. More than _____ people climb Mount Fuji each year.
5. _____ percent of the climbers are Japanese, and _____ percent come from foreign countries.
6. _____ and _____ are the best months to climb Mount Fuji.
7. People like to watch the _____ from the top of the mountain.

Understanding Sentences with *Because*

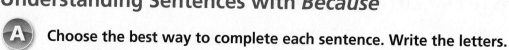 **Choose the best way to complete each sentence. Write the letters.**

_c_ **1.** People can see Mount Fuji from many parts of Japan

a. because it is dormant ("sleeping").

____ **2.** Artists draw and paint pictures of Mount Fuji

b. because the air is thin.

____ **3.** This volcano is safe to climb

c. because it's over 12,000 feet (3,776 meters) high.

____ **4.** July and August are the best months to climb Mount Fuji

d. because they want to be at the top at sunrise.

____ **5.** It's hard to breathe high on the mountain

e. because it has a beautiful shape.

____ **6.** Many people climb at night

f. because the weather is good then.

B **Complete this sentence:**

I (would / wouldn't) like to climb Mount Fuji because _____

_____ .

Summarizing

Some of the information in this summary of the reading is wrong. Find and correct six mistakes. The first mistake is corrected for you.

mountain

Mount Fuji is a beautiful ~~island~~ in Japan. It's famous for its unusual

history. More than 200,000 people drive to the top of it each year. July

and August are the dangerous months to climb it. Most of the climbers are

Japanese, but many come from Japan. Many climb the mountain at night

so they can paint the sunrise.

Sharing Opinions

Think about the questions. Then talk with a partner.

1. What does this statement mean: "A person who never climbs Mount Fuji is a fool"?

   a. Only crazy people climb Mount Fuji.

   b. Everybody should climb Mount Fuji.

   Do you agree? Tell why or why not.

2. What does this statement mean: "A person who climbs Mount Fuji twice is twice the fool"?

   a. Only crazy people climb Mount Fuji twice.

   b. Everybody should climb Mount Fuji twice.

   Do you agree? Tell why or why not.

3. Some people say, "Everybody should climb Mount Fuji at some time in his or her life." Think of something else that is worth doing. How would you complete this statement?

   Everybody should _____

   at some time in his or her life.

Using New Words

Work with a partner. Choose five target words or phrases from the list on page 66. On a piece of paper, use each word or phrase in a sentence.

Writing

Imagine that a foreign visitor to your country asks you, "Where should I go in your country? What should I see? What should I do?" Write six sentences. Begin each sentence:

I think you should . . .

UNIT 2 Wrap-up

REVIEWING VOCABULARY

A Match the words and phrases with their definitions. There are two extra words.

anywhere else	count	draw	land	temperature	twice
below	dangerous	✔ however	size	too much	

1. _____however_____ = but

2. _____ = in any other place

3. _____ = under, at a lower point or place

4. _____ = a measure of how hot or cold something is

5. _____ = a measure of how big or small something is

6. _____ = likely to hurt someone, not safe

7. _____ = tell how many there are of something (1, 2, 3, . . .)

8. _____ = more than is good or wanted

9. _____ = two times

B **Complete the sentences. There are two extra words.**

ahead	completely	foreign	imagine	probably	such as
belong to	find out	government	of course	rock	whole

1. He's inviting the _____ class to his house, all thirty people.

2. They'll _____ have cake at the birthday party. It's a tradition.

3. Lions, tigers, and house cats all _____ the cat family.

4. I don't know the answer. I will ask somebody and _____.

5. The bus is _____ full. No more people can get on it.

6. Many people from _____ countries visit San Marino.

7. _____ that you have one million dollars. Isn't that a nice idea?

8. Doctors tell us to eat fruit, _____ apples, oranges, and bananas.

9. The president is the most important person in the _____.

10. Is it cold in Antarctica? Well, _____ it is!

EXPANDING VOCABULARY

Word Families

Each form of a word belongs to the same **word family**. For example, the noun *student*, the verb *study*, and the adjective *studious* are all part of the same word family.

Sometimes two words in a word family look the same. See the chart below.

	Nouns	Verbs	Adjectives
1.	climb	climb	
2.		cool	cool
3.		empty	empty
4.	exercise	exercise	
5.	paint	paint	
6.	shape	shape	

 Look at the **boldfaced** words in the sentences below. What are they? Write *noun*, *verb*, or *adjective* above each word.

verb

1. **a.** Do you sometimes **climb** mountains?

   b. It's a long **climb** to the top of Mount Fuji.

2. **a.** You can **cool** your drink with some ice.

   b. Would you like a **cool** drink?

3. **a.** My cup is **empty**. I have no more coffee.

   b. Please **empty** the dishwasher.

4. **a.** Growing children need lots of **exercise**.

   b. Do you **exercise** three days a week?

5. **a.** My friends are going to **paint** their house.

   b. I'm planning to buy some blue **paint**.

6. **a.** He knows what kind of tree it is by the **shape** of its leaves.

   b. Things we see on TV often **shape** our opinions.

A PUZZLE

There are ten target words from Unit 2 in this puzzle. The words go across (→) and down (↓). Find the words and circle them. Use them to complete the sentences below.

H	I	S	T	O	R	Y	X	F	A
T	X	R	K	X	K	Q	Z	P	G
B	R	Z	Z	W	W	N	B	N	O
A	B	O	V	E	X	Z	E	V	O
S	C	I	E	N	T	I	S	T	N
X	V	Q	X	V	X	Z	T	B	C
W	Q	Z	B	R	E	A	T	H	E
Z	X	S	T	O	N	E	X	M	Z
Q	W	K	J	O	N	L	Y	V	K
F	M	V	X	F	P	M	B	K	H

Across

1. Call the doctor if the child's temperature goes _____ 102 degrees.
2. Children study the _____ of their country in school.
3. There aren't many continents,_____ seven.
4. Their house is made of _____.
5. He is a _____. He studies the oceans.
6. It's not healthy to _____ smoke from cigarettes.

Down

7. Here are three pictures by that artist. Which is the _____ picture?
8. Their plane is here. It arrived ten minutes _____.
9. I go food shopping _____ a week, on Saturday.
10. There's a hole in the _____ of the house, and rain is coming in.

BUILDING DICTIONARY SKILLS

A Dictionaries use many **abbreviations**. An abbreviation is a short way to write a word. What do these abbreviations mean? Check your answers in your dictionary.

1. P.O. _Post Office_   3. yd. _____   5. Jr. _____

2. St. _____   4. DJ _____   6. F _____

B Dictionaries often use abbreviations for **parts of speech**. Parts of speech are categories of words, such as nouns, verbs, and adjectives.

1. Look at the dictionary entries below. Find the abbreviations for *noun*, *verb*, and *adjective*. Circle them.

---

pro•tect /prə'tɛkt/ *v* [T] to prevent someone or something from being harmed or damaged: *a lotion to **protect** you **from** sunburn* | *a plan to **protect** the town **against** another attack*
 –**protected** *adj: a protected species*
 –**protector** *n: a chest protector*
pro•tec•tion /prə'tɛkʃən/ *n* **1** [U] the act of protecting, or the state of being protected: *Heidi's thin coat **gave** little **protection against** the cold.* **2** [singular] something that protects someone or something: *A car alarm **provides/gives** some protection **against** theft.*
pro•tec•tive /prə'tɛktɪv/ *adj* **1** used or intended for protection: *a protective covering for the computer* **2** wanting to protect . . .

---

2. Look at your own dictionary. Does it use abbreviations for *noun*, *verb*, and *adjective*?

☐ No, it doesn't.   ☐ Yes, it does. They are _____, _____, and _____.

C These words are related to target words from Unit 2. What parts of speech are they? Write the abbreviation *n.*, *v.*, or *adj.*

1. actual   _adj._

ac•tu•al /'æktʃuəl, 'ækʃuəl/ *adj* real, especially when compared with what is believed, expected, or intended: *Were those his actual words?*

2. collector _____

col•lec•tor /kə'lɛktɚ/ *n* **1** someone whose job is to collect things: *a tax collector* **2** someone who collects things for pleasure: *a rock collector*

3. shiny _____

4. stranger _____

strang•er /'streɪndʒɚ/ *n* [C] **1** someone you do not know: *Never talk to strangers.* | *a phone call from a **total/perfect/complete stranger*** **2** someone in a new and unfamiliar . . .

shin•y /'ʃaɪni/ *adj* bright and smooth looking: *shiny hair* | *shiny leather boots*

Vocabulary Self-Test 1

Circle the letter of the word or phrase that best completes each sentence.

Example: The sun goes down in the _____.

    a. artist   **b.** race   **c.** west   **d.** result

1. It's always warm there. The temperature never goes _____ 60°F.

    a. twice   **b.** below   **c.** completely   **d.** ago

2. You should ask your doctor questions about your _____.

    a. health   **b.** roof   **c.** government   **d.** island

3. Wear a hat to _____ yourself from the sun.

    a. climb   **b.** protect   **c.** shine   **d.** collect

4. His story was true. _____, nobody believed him.

    a. Else   **b.** Such as   **c.** However   **d.** Especially

5. It is _____ to walk alone in this city at night. Don't do it.

    a. basic   **b.** foreign   **c.** dangerous   **d.** nervous

6. He always shows great _____ for his mother and father.

    a. age   **b.** size   **c.** respect   **d.** temperature

7. Antarctica looks small on the map, but it is _____ bigger than Australia.

    a. second   **b.** percent   **c.** above   **d.** actually

8. Everyone studies the _____ of their country in school.

    a. stone   **b.** history   **c.** surprise   **d.** distance

9. Baghdad is the _____ of Iraq.

    a. capital   **b.** education   **c.** scientist   **d.** continent

10. You'll have to wait a _____ for the results of the test.

    a. land   **b.** shape   **c.** while   **d.** mind

11. The runners are _____ the race. It will be fun.

    a. spelling   **b.** drawing   **c.** painting   **d.** looking forward to

12. The weather _____ cool at the end of the summer.
   a. imagines   **b.** gets   **c.** takes   **d.** practices

13. People often use dictionaries to _____ the meanings of new words.
   a. describe   **b.** look up   **c.** of course   **d.** go on

14. Children need _____, so they should go out and play.
   a. luck   **b.** style   **c.** tradition   **d.** exercise

15. Eggs, milk, and cheese are just a few of the _____ of their farm.
   a. products   **b.** beaches   **c.** races   **d.** opinions

16. People can go online to find _____ about history.
   a. facts   **b.** rocks   **c.** mountains   **d.** skills

17. Those two kinds of chocolate are good, but this one is the _____.
   a. whole   **b.** simple   **c.** worth   **d.** best

18. The islands of the Galápagos _____ Ecuador.
   a. would like   **b.** travel   **c.** belong to   **d.** find out

19. The air is so cold that it hurts to _____.
   a. breathe   **b.** add   **c.** give up   **d.** become

20. She does not use her parents' car. She has her _____ car.
   a. own   **b.** soft   **c.** shy   **d.** alone

21. He is always saying _____ things. No one understands him.
   a. favorite   **b.** another   **c.** empty   **d.** strange

22. If the child's mother isn't home, then _____ her father? Is he home?
   a. what about   **b.** such as   **c.** too much   **d.** probably

23. I got interested in the idea of traveling to Antarctica _____ five years ago.
   a. enough   **b.** several   **c.** about   **d.** tiny

24. He's good at table tennis. He plays the game very _____.
   a. sweet   **b.** well   **c.** crazy   **d.** only

25. Texas is a big state, but Alaska is _____ bigger.
   a. even   **b.** once   **c.** unusual   **d.** each other

See the Answer Key on page 207.

OUR BODIES

Your Sense of Taste

Mmm, this tastes good!

GETTING READY TO READ

Talk with a partner.

1. a. What tastes good to you? On a piece of paper, write a list of your favorite things to eat and drink. (Write fast! You have one minute.)

    b. Show your list to your partner. On your lists, circle the things you both like.

2. a. What do you **not** like to eat or drink? Write another list. (Write fast! You have 30 seconds.)

    b. Show your list to your partner. Circle any food or drink that is on both your lists.

3. What did you learn about your partner's likes and dislikes?

READING

Look at the words and pictures next to the reading. Then read without stopping. Don't worry about new words. Don't stop to use a dictionary. Just keep reading!

Your Sense of Taste

1 **Taste** is one of our five **senses**. The other four are hearing, **sight**, smell, and **touch**. We hear with our ears, we see with our eyes, we smell with our nose, and we feel things with our whole body. Our sense of taste **depends** mostly on our tongue.[1]

[1] a *tongue*

2 On the tongue, there are groups of tiny taste buds. Taste buds send information about food to the **brain**. We have a lot of taste buds, maybe even 10,000. People do not all have the same number of them. Women often have more taste buds than men.

[2] Lemons are *sour*.

3 Because of our taste buds, foods like ice cream and bananas taste sweet. French fries, cheese, and ocean water taste **salty**. Lemons have a sour[2] taste, and coffee is bitter.[3] Most people know about these four main tastes: sweet, salty, sour, and bitter. But scientists now know about a fifth taste: umami. We can find it in some kinds of cheese, meat, and mushrooms.[4] *Umami* is a Japanese word. It means something like "good-tasting."

[3] Coffee or hot chocolate without sugar is *bitter*.

[4] *mushrooms*

4 People can lose their sense of taste. For example, if you have a cold and cannot breathe **through** your nose, then it is hard to taste food. Different foods may all taste the same. This happens because there is a close **relationship** between our sense of taste and our sense of smell. Each sense **affects** the other.

5 The temperature of food also affects its taste. Tastes are not as strong in very hot or very cold foods. For example, very cold, hard ice cream is not as sweet as not-so-cold, soft ice cream. Also, sometimes a food tastes good only at the right temperature. **Consider** your favorite cold drink. Does it **still** taste good when it is not cold? Many people love cold Coca-Cola but **cannot stand** it warm.

(continued)

6   Why does a sense of taste **matter**? For one thing, it helps people make **decisions** about what is and is not safe to eat. And of course, thanks to[5] your sense of taste, you can enjoy everything on your list of favorite things to eat and drink.

[5] *thanks to* = because of

Quick Comprehension Check

Read these sentences about the reading. Circle T (true) or F (false).

1. People have five senses: taste, hearing, sight, smell, and touch.   T   F

2. We need our tongue to taste things.   T   F

3. Taste buds send information about food to your stomach.   T   F

4. There are only four main tastes: sweet, salty, sour, and bitter.   T   F

5. Our sense of taste can change.   T   F

6. The temperature of food can be important to how it tastes.   T   F

EXPLORING VOCABULARY

Thinking about the Target Vocabulary

 A   Find the words and phrases in **bold** in "Your Sense of Taste" on pages 81 and 82. Write them in the list in alphabetical order.

1. affects	6.	11.
2. brain	7.	12.
3.	8.	13.
4.	9.	14.
5.	10.	15.

 B   Which words and phrases are new to you? Circle them here. Then find them in the reading. Look at the context. Can you guess the meaning?

Using the Target Vocabulary

 A **Complete these sentences. Use the nouns** *brain, ears, eyes, nose,* *senses, sight, smell,* **and** *taste.* **Use the verbs** *taste* **and** *smell.*

1. Tom has five _____senses_____ : hearing, touch, _____,
   _____, and _____.

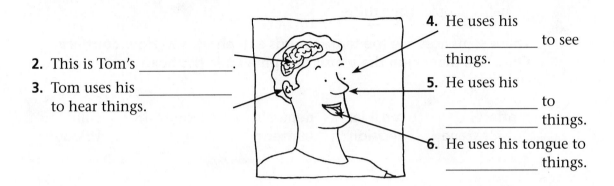

2. This is Tom's _____.

3. Tom uses his _____
   to hear things.

4. He uses his
   _____ to see
   things.

5. He uses his
   _____ to
   _____ things.

6. He uses his tongue to
   _____ things.

B **These sentences are about the reading. Complete them with the** **words and phrases in the box.**

affects	consider	depends	relationship	still
cannot stand	decisions	matters	salty	through

1. You need your tongue to taste things. Your sense of taste
   _____ on your tongue.

2. Ocean water and many kinds of cheese have a _____
   taste.

3. Your sense of smell _____, or changes, the way food
   tastes.

4. When you breathe, air goes in and out _____ your nose.

5. Your sense of smell affects your sense of taste. There's a close
   _____ between these two senses.

6. Some foods taste good at only one temperature. Others taste good
   hot, and they _____ taste good when they get cold.

7. When you _____ something, you think about it, especially before you decide what to do.

8. Many people like Coca-Cola when it's cold. But do they still like it when it's warm? No! They _____ it!

9. A sense of taste is important. It _____.

10. People have to decide what is and is not safe to eat. The sense of taste helps people make those _____.

C   These sentences use the target words and phrases **in new contexts**. Complete them with the words and phrases in the box.

affects	consider	depends	relationship	still
can't stand	decision	matter	salty	through

1. Bob and Mary are happily married. They have a good _____.

2. I never read history books. I _____ them. They put me to sleep.

3. I need something to drink. This pizza is very _____.

4. The weather often _____ the work on a farm.

5. They might not play the baseball game today. It _____ on the weather.

6. He didn't have his house key, so he climbed in _____ a window.

7. We can go down Main Street or Park Avenue. It doesn't _____. It's the same distance both ways.

8. His work is dangerous. He should _____ getting a new job.

9. Should we go out or stay in? Let's make a _____.

10. He is seventy-five years old, but he won't give up running. He _____ runs every day.

Word Grammar: *Taste*

There is more than one way to use the word *taste*. *Taste* can be:

- a noun *Smoking affects a person's sense of **taste**.*

  *He doesn't like the **taste** of broccoli.*

- a verb *The pizza **tastes** great!*

  *Come and **taste** the soup. Does it need more salt?*

Write two sentences with *taste*. Use it as both a noun and a verb.

1. _____

2. _____

DEVELOPING YOUR SKILLS

Topics of Paragraphs

 Look at the list of paragraph topics from "Your Sense of Taste." Find the paragraph on each topic in the reading. Write the paragraph number (1–6).

a. five tastes of food   Paragraph __3__

b. our five senses   Paragraph ____

c. why a sense of taste matters   Paragraph ____

d. tastes and temperatures   Paragraph ____

e. our taste buds   Paragraph ____

f. the relationship between the senses of
   taste and smell   Paragraph ____

B   Write a sentence about each of the six topics from paragraphs 1–6. Use information from the reading.

1. The five senses are taste, touch, hearing, sight, and smell.

2. _____

3. _____

4. _____

5. _____

6. _____

Summarizing

A   These six sentences form a summary of the reading. Number the sentences in order.

_____ **a.** The others are hearing, touch, sight, and smell.

_____ **b.** The taste buds on it send information to your brain.

__1__ **c.** Taste is one of our five senses.

_____ **d.** You can taste things because of your tongue.

_____ **e.** For example, your sense of smell and the temperature of the food can do this.

_____ **f.** Several things can affect the taste of food.

B   Write the sentences in Part A as a paragraph.

_____

_____

_____

_____

_____

_____

_____

Sharing Opinions

A Which of the five senses is most important to you? Write the number 1 next to it in the chart. Which one is least important? Write the number 5 next to it. Number the other senses in order of importance.

B Talk with two or three others in a small group. Find out their opinions. Complete the chart.

The Five Senses	You	(name)	(name)	(name)
The sense of hearing				
The sense of sight				
The sense of smell				
The sense of taste				
The sense of touch				

Using New Words

Work alone or with a partner. Choose five target words and phrases from the list on page 82. On a piece of paper, use each word or phrase in a sentence.

Writing

Sometimes the taste or smell of something makes us remember a place or a person. Write a paragraph about a taste or smell like that. You can begin: *The (smell/taste) of _____ makes me think of* . . . Write four or more sentences.

CHAPTER 10

Bones

Why is his arm in a sling?

GETTING READY TO READ

Talk with a partner or in a small group.

1. On a piece of paper, make a list of names for parts of the body (*head*, *legs*, *eyes*, . . .). Write fast! You have one minute.

2. Look at your list. Which parts of the body have bones in them? Circle them.

3. How many bones are there in your body?

    a. 102   **b.** 145   **c.** 206

4. How many joints[1] are there in your body?

    a. under 50   **b.** over 70   **c.** over 100

[1] A *joint* is where two bones come together.

88

READING

Look at the words and picture next to the reading. Then read without stopping.

Bones

1   Imagine your body with no **bones**. It is not a pretty picture,[1] is it?

2   We need our bones. They **support** our bodies so we can stand. They also protect soft parts inside us. For example, your skull[2] protects your brain. Your ribs[2] protect your **heart**.

3   The bones in your body **make up** your skeleton.[2] Your skeleton has long bones (in your arms and legs) and short bones (such as the bones in your fingers). It has some very tiny bones, too. (They are in the part of your ear inside your head). So, how many bones do you have in all? There are 206 of them.

4   In many places, two bones come together. There are joints at these places. Your **knees** are the joints in the **middle** of your legs. Your **elbows** are the joints in the middle of your arms. You need joints to move your arms, legs, neck, and back. The **human** body has more than seventy joints.

5   Your elbow and your **shoulder** are examples of two different **types** of joints. Your arm can bend at the elbow, but it can bend just one way. At the shoulder, your arm can move freely up, down, left, right, and all around. There are other types of joints, too. For example, babies have joints between the eight bones that make up the skull. Then these bones grow together, so in older children and **adults**, the joints do not move.

6   Sometimes people have problems with their joints, especially older adults. Doctors have ways to **fix** many of these problems. They can even put in a new knee or hip.[3] These artificial[4] joints are usually **metal** or **plastic**. Doctors can also fix bones that break. But it is best to keep your skeleton in good health! Are you **taking care of** yours?

[1] *not a pretty picture* = not nice to look at or think about

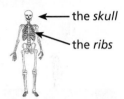
the *skull*
the *ribs*

[2] a human *skeleton*

[3] a *hip* = the joint where the leg connects to the main part of the body

[4] *artificial* = not natural, made by people

Quick Comprehension Check

 A Read these sentences about the reading. Circle T (true) or F (false).

1. There are about 100 bones in the human body.   T   F

2. Bones hold up our bodies so we can stand.   T   F

3. Bones come together at joints.   T   F

4. We have joints to protect the soft parts inside our bodies.   T   F

5. There are different kinds of joints.   T   F

6. Doctors use old bones to make new joints.   T   F

B Look back at the questions in **Getting Ready to Read** on page 88. Check your answers.

EXPLORING VOCABULARY

Thinking about the Target Vocabulary

 A Find the words and phrases in **bold** in "Bones" on page 89. Write them in the list in alphabetical order.

1. adults   6.   11.

2. bones   7.   12.

3.   8.   13.

4.   9.   14.

5.   10.   15.

B Which words and phrases are new to you? Circle them here. Then find them in the reading. Look at the context. Can you guess the meaning?

Using the Target Vocabulary

 A **Complete the sentence. Then label the picture. Write** *bones*, *elbow*, *human*, *joints*, *knee*, **or** *shoulder*.

1. The _____ body has 206 _____.

2. _____

3. _____

4. _____

5. _____

B **These sentences are about the reading. Complete them with the words and phrases in the box.**

adults	heart	metal	plastic	taking care of
fix	make up	middle	support	types

1. We depend on our bones to _____ our bodies. They hold us up.

2. The _____ is a very important part of the human body. If it stops, the person usually dies.

3. The bones in a person's body _____ his or her skeleton. Together, they form the skeleton.

4. Your elbows are the joints in the _____ of your arms. They are at the center, or the halfway point, in your arms.

5. There are several different kinds of joints. Your elbows and shoulders are two different _____ of joints.

6. Babies have joints between the bones of their skulls. The skulls of babies are different from the skulls of _____.

7. People sometimes break bones, or they have problems with their joints. Doctors then try to _____ the bone or the joint.

8. Doctors sometimes put in a new joint made of _____.
This is a hard, usually shiny material. Knives and forks are usually made of some type of this material.

9. Some new joints are made of _____ because it is easy to form it into different shapes. This material is used for credit cards, shopping bags, and toothbrushes.

10. Are you _____ your bones? What can you do to protect them?

C **These sentences use the target words and phrases in new contexts. Complete them with the words and phrases in the box.**

adult	heart	metal	plastic	takes care of
fixes	makes up	middle	support	type

1. Sometimes I don't sleep well. I wake up in the _____ of the night.

2. At what age does a young person become an _____?

3. The walls of a house _____ the roof.

4. What _____ of exercise do you like best?

5. Water _____ two-thirds (²/₃) of the human body.

6. Sometimes Eva and Don are both at work. Then a babysitter _____ their children.

7. Ed is an automobile mechanic. He works at a garage and he _____ cars.

8. Some car parts are plastic, but car engines are made of _____.

9. People buy soda in clear _____ or glass bottles and shiny metal cans.

10. Running makes your _____ work harder.

Word Grammar: The Parts of Speech

> Nouns, verbs, and adjectives are some of the different kinds, or categories, of words. Each kind of word has a different use. All the different kinds of words are called **the parts of speech**.

A Label each list of words. Write: *Adjectives*, *Verbs*, or *Nouns*.

1. _____	2. _____	3. _____
artist	affect	best
beach	count	cool
brain	depend	human
decision	paint	lucky
shoulder	receive	salty
_____	_____	_____
_____	_____	_____
_____	_____	_____
_____	_____	_____
_____	_____	_____

B Add these words to the chart in Part A: *adult, consider, dangerous, emergency, fix, unusual.*

C Add two or more words of your own to each category in Part A.

DEVELOPING YOUR SKILLS

Scanning

Read these questions about "Bones." Scan the reading, and write short answers.

1. Why do we need our bones? Give two reasons. _____

    _____

2. How many bones are in the human skeleton? _____

3. Where in the body can you find tiny bones? _____

4. How many joints are there? _____

5. What are two examples of different kinds of joints? _____

_____

6. What is one difference between babies and adults? _____

_____

7. What are artificial joints made of? _____

Topics of Paragraphs

A Look at the list of paragraph topics from "Bones." Find the paragraph on each topic in the reading. Write the paragraph number (1–6).

a. care of bones and joints   Paragraph ____

b. why we need our bones   Paragraph ____

c. your body without bones   Paragraph ____

d. joints in the human body   Paragraph ____

e. types of joints   Paragraph ____

f. bones of the human skeleton   Paragraph ____

B Write a sentence about each of the topics from paragraphs 2–6. Use information from the reading.

Paragraph 2: *Our bones support our bodies and protect soft body parts.*

Paragraph 3: _____

Paragraph 4: _____

Paragraph 5: _____

Paragraph 6: _____

Discussion

 Read the questions in the chart below. Write *yes* or *no* or put a
question mark (?) if you don't know.

Taking Care of Your Bones	You	_____ (name)	_____ (name)
1. Do you eat enough foods with calcium (from milk, cheese, yogurt, ice cream) for strong bones?			
2. Do you get enough vitamin D (from milk or sunlight)?			
3. Do you get enough exercise?			
4. Do you usually eat well?			
5. Is it hard for you to eat the right foods?			

 Talk with two other people about the questions in the chart. Find out
their answers. Complete the chart and talk about your answers with
the class.

Using New Words

Ask and answer these questions with a partner. Use one of the words
in parentheses. Then talk about your answers with the class.

1. Can you name five **types** of (fruit/animals)?
2. Can you name three things made of (**metal/plastic**)?
3. Do you ever fall asleep in the **middle** of a (movie/class)?
4. When does a (girl/boy) become an **adult**?

Writing

You know it's important to have a good diet (to eat well) for strong
bones and a healthy body. Do you think it's hard to eat well? Are you
happy with your diet? Is there anything you would like to change?
Write a paragraph of five or more sentences about eating well. You can
begin: *My diet these days is (good / OK / bad)*.

Giving Blood

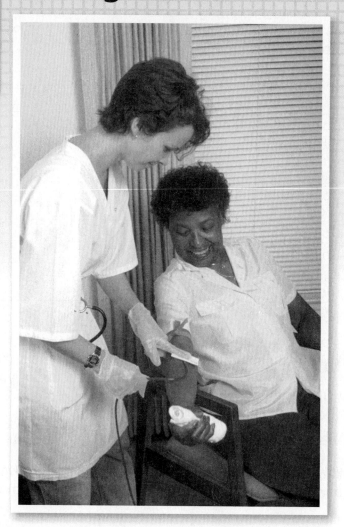

Giving blood

GETTING READY TO READ

Talk about these questions with your class.

1. What do you see in the photo?
2. Do you know any people who give blood?
3. There are four main types of blood. How many people in the class know their own blood type?

   _____ out of _____ people
      (total)

READING

Look at the words next to the reading. Then read without stopping.

Giving Blood

1   Some people cannot stand the sight of **blood**. They hate to see their own blood, and they do not want to look at anyone else's blood, **either**!

2   Liz Kim does not **mind** the sight of blood. She is **used to** it. Liz is a **nurse**, and she sees blood every day. She works in a U.S. hospital. It is her job to take blood from blood donors.[1]

3   Hospitals **store** blood in blood banks. "Hospitals need to have blood ready for **emergencies**," says Liz. "People may need blood for a lot of **reasons**. For example, someone might be in a car **accident** and need blood. Or a doctor might have to give a **patient** a blood transfusion[2] during surgery.[3] Here in the U.S., one out of ten patients in the hospital needs a transfusion."

4   Any new blood must be a good **match** for the patient's own blood type. The four main blood types are A, B, AB, and O.

- People with type A can donate[4] blood to people with type A or AB.

- People with type B can donate to people with B or AB.

- People with type AB can donate only to other people with AB. However, they can **receive** A, B, AB, or O type blood. They're **lucky**.

- Type O blood is **special**. This is the blood type that hospitals want most. People with type O can give blood to anyone. But they can **accept** blood only from other people with type O.

[1] a *blood donor* = a person who gives blood for free

[2] a *blood transfusion* = the act of putting new blood into someone's body

[3] *surgery* = the act of cutting into someone's body to fix something

[4] *donate* = give (to a person or group that needs help)

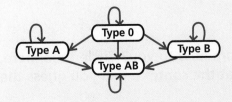

(continued)

5   Not many people give blood. In the United States, only one out of twenty adults gives blood. In many countries, even fewer adults do. Some people cannot give blood for health reasons. Others are too nervous. Liz Kim thinks most people just never consider it. "Giving blood helps others," she says. "It's also good for your heart. Please, think about it!"

Quick Comprehension Check

Read these sentences about the reading. Circle T (true) or F (false).

1. It is hard for Liz Kim to look at blood.   T   F

2. There are four main types of blood.   T   F

3. A person's blood type doesn't matter at all.   T   F

4. Everyone can give blood to everyone else.   T   F

5. Most adults in the United States give blood.   T   F

6. Liz Kim wants more people to give blood.   T   F

EXPLORING VOCABULARY

Thinking about the Target Vocabulary

A Find the words and phrases in **bold** in "Giving Blood" on page 97. Write them in the list in alphabetical order.

1. accept	6.	11.
2. accident	7.	12.
3.	8.	13.
4.	9.	14.
5.	10.	15.

B Which words and phrases are new to you? Circle them here. Then find them in the reading. Look at the context. Can you guess the meaning?

Using the Target Vocabulary

 These sentences are **about the reading.** Complete them with the words and phrase in the box.

either	lucky	mind	receive	store
emergency	match	nurse	special	used to

1. Some people can't stand the sight of their own blood. They don't want to see anyone else's blood, _____.

2. For other people, the sight of blood isn't so bad. It doesn't really matter to them. They don't _____ it.

3. Liz Kim sees blood all the time. Liz is _____ the sight of blood. It's not new or strange to her.

4. The job of a _____ is taking care of sick or hurt people.

5. Hospitals keep blood in blood banks. A blood bank is a place to _____ blood.

6. Sometimes a person is hurt and loses a lot of blood. He or she needs new blood fast. This is an example of an _____.

7. Any new blood has to go together well with a person's own blood. It has to be a good _____ for their own blood.

8. Blood donors give blood. Hospitals _____ blood from donors.

9. People with type AB blood can receive type A, B, AB, or O. When they need blood, it's easy to find, so they're _____.

10. People with type O blood can give it to anyone. In this way, type O is different from the other types. It's good for hospitals to have it. Type O blood is _____.

These sentences use the target words and phrase **in new contexts.**
Complete them with the words and phrase in the box.

either	lucky	mind	receives	store
emergency	match	nurse	special	used to

1. Do you _____ if I sit here?

2. Ralph's orange tie is not a good _____ for his green shirt.

3. On her birthday, Nancy _____ cards and presents from her friends.

4. Susan has a bad cut on her hand. We have to take her to the _____ room at the hospital.

5. I don't want to do the same old thing tonight. Let's do something _____.

6. That fish soup doesn't look good, and it doesn't smell good, _____.

7. My parents are nervous about flying, but my brothers and I often travel by plane. We are _____ it.

8. Students can get health information from the school _____.

9. Alan was in a car accident, but he wasn't hurt. He was _____.

10. We use computers to _____ information.

C Read these sentences. Match the **boldfaced** target words with their definitions.

a. I tried to give the driver some money, but he wouldn't **accept** it.

b. Even careful drivers sometimes have car **accidents**.

c. The doctor's waiting room is full of **patients**.

d. Mark sometimes leaves work early without giving any **reason**.

e. Donna cut her hand on some glass, and there was a lot of **blood**.

Target Words   **Definitions**

1. _____ = the cause of something (why it happens)

2. _____ = the red liquid that moves through your body

3. _____ = agree to do or take something

4. _____ = people who get care from a doctor or nurse

5. _____ = things that go wrong, bad things that happen by mistake

Word Grammar: *Too* vs. *Either*

Too can mean "also." For example:

*My elbow hurts, and my shoulder hurts, **too**.*

*Doctors help patients, and nurses do, **too**.*

Use *either*, not *too*, in negative sentences. For example:

*Jack's **not** here, and Sam isn't, **either**.*

*My knees don't hurt, and my feet don't, **either**.*

Complete these sentences. Use *too* or *either*.

1. A cold can affect your breathing and your sense of smell,

   _____.

2. He's not nervous, and she isn't, _____.

3. I can't buy a new car or a used one, _____.

4. I like the shape of that car and the color, _____.

5. I can't climb that mountain, and you can't, _____.

6. He's taking history courses, and he's studying foreign languages,

   _____.

7. His brother can fix cars and motorcycles, _____.

8. That girl doesn't eat well, and her friends don't, _____.

DEVELOPING YOUR SKILLS

Understanding Sentences with *Because*

A   **Choose the best way to complete each sentence. Write the letters.**

___d___ **1.** Liz Kim doesn't mind the sight of blood

_____ **2.** She sees blood every day

_____ **3.** Hospitals must have blood ready

_____ **4.** You can't receive just anyone's blood

_____ **5.** Type O blood is special

_____ **6.** People with type AB are lucky

a. because new blood must match your own.

b. because people with any blood type can use it.

c. because she works with blood donors.

d. because she's used to it.

e. because they can accept type A, B, AB, or O.

f. because patients may need it.

B   **Complete this sentence.**

People give blood because _____.

Summarizing

A   **These seven sentences make up a summary of the reading. Number the sentences in order.**

_____ **a.** The blood they give is stored in the hospital blood bank.

_____ **b.** For example, people with type O blood can accept only type O.

___1___ **c.** Liz Kim is a hospital nurse.

_____ **d.** The blood that patients receive must be a good match for their own blood.

_____ **e.** She takes blood from donors.

___7___ **f.** Liz wants more people to give blood.

_____ **g.** The blood bank keeps it for patients who need a transfusion.

B Write the sentences in Part A as a paragraph.

_____

_____

_____

_____

_____

_____

Discussion

Talk about these questions with a partner.

1. How do you complete this diagram? Write *A*, *B*, *AB*, and *O*. What does the diagram say?

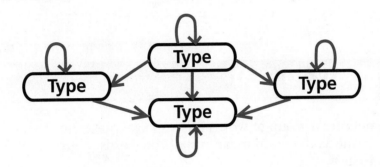

2. How do you feel about giving blood? Discuss your ideas and feelings. Then share them with the class.

Using New Words

Work with a partner. Take turns asking for and giving information. Then tell the class something about your partner.

1. Tell me who you would call in different types of **emergencies**.
2. Tell me a kind of present you like to **receive**.
3. Tell me something that's new in your life and hard for you to **get used to**.
4. Tell me about a **special** person in your life.

Writing

Does a nurse have a good job or a bad job? Write a paragraph about nurses and their work. You can begin: *Nurses have _____ jobs.* Give the reasons for your opinion.

CHAPTER 12

Can You Give Me a Hand?

GETTING READY TO READ

Sometimes a group of words has a special meaning. This meaning is not the same as the usual meanings of the words. A group of words like this is an **idiom**.

A Which four sentences below do you think have idioms? Check (✓) them.

__✔__ **1.** He wants a shoulder to cry on.

_____ **2.** He'll give you a hand.

_____ **3.** He needs to wash his hands.

_____ **4.** The teacher has eyes in the back of his head.

_____ **5.** The teacher is keeping an eye on the students.

B Match the idioms in Part A with their meanings. Write the numbers.

__4__ **a.** He sees everything that happens in class.

_____ **b.** He wants someone to listen to his problems.

_____ **c.** He will help you.

_____ **d.** He's watching the students.

READING

Look at the words and picture next to the reading. Then read without stopping.

Can You Give Me a Hand?

1   An **idiom** is a group of words with a special meaning. The words in the idiom do not have their **usual** meanings. Together, the words mean something else **instead**. You know some idioms **already**, and you will need to learn more. English is full of idioms.

2   Many idioms **mention** parts of the body: the head, the hands, the heart, **and so on**. For example, someone could say, "My sister Lisa is getting a big head." Lisa's head is not growing. *A big head* is an idiom. A person with a big head thinks that he or she is very important and special. Lisa's brother or sister is saying, "Lisa is starting to think too much of herself."

3   A friend could say, "Be careful. Bill has a big mouth."[1] Your friend is not saying that Bill's mouth is large. *Have a big mouth* is an idiom. Your friend means that Bill says too much. He tells other people's **secrets**. Your friend is giving you some **advice**: You should not tell Bill any **private** information. You cannot **trust** him to keep quiet.[2]

4   Take a guess at the meanings of these three sentences. Each sentence has an idiom. Each idiom mentions the heart, but they have nothing to do with[3] the heart.

   1. She knows the words to that song by heart.
   2. My heart was in my mouth.
   3. He has a heart of **gold**.

Did you **figure out** the meanings of the sentences? Here they are:

   1. She can remember the words to that song very well.
   2. I was very afraid.
   3. He is very good and **kind** to other people.

(continued)

[1] a *mouth*

[2] *keep quiet* = keep information secret

[3] *have nothing to do with* = have no relationship to

5   There are idioms in every language. Some idioms in your first language may be the same in English. If so, the meaning in English will be **clear**. For example, for some Spanish speakers, the idiom *a heart of gold* is the same in Spanish: *un corazón de oro*.

6   The meaning of an idiom is not always easy to guess. So **perhaps** you will want to buy a dictionary of idioms. That might be a good idea. Just do not pay an arm and a leg for it.

Quick Comprehension Check

Read these sentences about the reading. Circle T (true) or F (false).

1. An idiom is a group of words with a special meaning.   T   F

2. There are only a few idioms in English.   T   F

3. The idiom *have a big mouth* means "eat a lot."   T   F

4. A person with a heart of gold is very nervous.   T   F

5. Sometimes an idiom is the same in two languages.   T   F

6. You cannot find idioms in a dictionary.   T   F

EXPLORING VOCABULARY

Thinking about the Target Vocabulary

 Find the words and phrases in bold in "Can You Give Me a Hand?" on pages 105 and 106. Write them in the list in alphabetical order.

1. advice	6.	11.
2. already	7.	12.
3.	8.	13.
4.	9.	14.
5.	10.	15.

Which words and phrases are new to you? Circle them here. Then find them in the reading. Look at the context. Can you guess the meaning?

Using the Target Vocabulary

 These sentences are **about the reading**. Complete them with the words and phrase in the box.

already	figure out	idiom	secrets	usual
clear	gold	mention	trust	

1. Sometimes a group of words has a special meaning. For example, *have a sweet tooth* isn't about teeth. It means "like to eat sweet things." It's an _____.
2. The words in an idiom do not have their _____ meanings. They have a special meaning.
3. You have learned some idioms—you learned them at some time in the past—so you _____ know some idioms.
4. Many English idioms _____ parts of the body such as the eyes or hands, for example.
5. Sometimes we don't tell other people about an idea or a plan, or we quietly tell just a few people. Ideas or plans like these are _____.
6. You should tell secrets only to people you _____. Those are people you believe are good and honest, who will not do anything to hurt you.
7. You could say someone *has a heart of* _____. This special kind of metal is worth a lot of money.
8. Take time to think about something, and maybe then you can understand it. Sometimes, however, you just can't _____ the meaning of an idiom.
9. The meanings of some idioms are easy to understand. When the meaning isn't _____, try your dictionary.

B **These sentences use the target words and phrase in new contexts. Complete them with the words and phrase in the box.**

already	figure out	idiom	secret	usual
clear	gold	mention	trust	

1. Coins are made of different metals, such as silver and
   _____.

2. My math homework is very difficult. I'll need help to
   _____ the problems.

3. Don't tell anyone about their relationship. They want to keep it a
   _____.

4. There's a story in the newspaper about the boy's accident, but the
   story doesn't _____ the boy's name.

5. Why do you need a new computer? You _____ have a
   good one.

6. This cookbook tells how to make bread. There are pictures, too. So
   the way to make bread is very _____.

7. Don't believe anything he says. You can't _____ him.

8. Tomorrow's class will not begin at the _____ time. We'll
   start fifteen minutes late.

9. My guess is that *put your foot in your mouth* is an _____.

C **Read these sentences. Match the boldfaced target words and phrase with their definitions.**

a. Who does the cooking, cleaning, **and so on** in your family?

b. A **private** room in a hospital costs a lot.

c. He won't listen to me, but **perhaps** he'll take your **advice**.

d. Thanks for your help. It was very **kind** of you.

e. I don't have a pen, so can I use a pencil **instead**?

Target Words and Phrase	Definitions
1. _____	= maybe
2. _____	= nice, friendly, and helpful
3. _____	= an opinion or idea about what someone should do
4. _____	= in place of something or someone else
5. _____	= and other things of the same kind
6. _____	= not shared with other people

Word Grammar: Phrasal Verbs

Figure out is a **phrasal verb**. Phrasal verbs have two parts: a verb (such as *make, get,* or *turn*) and a particle (such as *up, out,* or *off*). The meaning of the phrasal verb is different from the meanings of its two parts. For example, *Please go on reading* does not mean to go anywhere, and *It's time for you to give up* does not mean you should give anything.

A Complete each sentence with a phrasal verb. Use *figure out, find out, give up, go on, look up,* or *make up.*

1. You can _____ words in a dictionary.
2. Foreign students _____ 15 percent of the Class of 2012.
3. I hope the party upstairs doesn't _____ all night!
4. I tried and tried, but I can't fix it. I'm sorry, but I _____.
5. What's happening across the street? Let's go and _____.
6. His writing is not clear. I can't _____ what his note says.

B **Write your own sentences with the phrasal verbs in Part A.**

1. _____

2. _____

3. _____

4. _____

5. _____

6. _____

DEVELOPING YOUR SKILLS

Scanning

Read these questions about "Can You Give Me a Hand?" Scan the reading, and write short answers.

1. What's an idiom? _____

2. What do many English idioms mention? _____

3. What does the idiom *have a big mouth* mean? _____
_____

4. Complete these idioms and their definitions:
   a. know something _____ = _____ something well
   b. have your heart in your _____ = be _____
   c. have a heart _____ = be a _____ person

Sentences with *Because*

Complete the sentences. Use information from the reading.

1. Learners of English need to know about idioms because _____
_____.

2. If someone has a big mouth, you shouldn't tell him or her anything
   private because _____.

3. It might be a good idea to get a dictionary of idioms because _____
_____.

Discussion

Talk about these questions in a small group or with the whole class.

1. Is "getting a big head" a good thing or a bad thing? Tell why.
2. The reading says "do not pay an arm and a leg" for a dictionary of idioms. What do you think that means?
3. What do you think *have a heart of stone* means?
4. Does your dictionary give you any help with idioms? Look up the word *heart* in your dictionary. Does it mention any idioms with *heart*?

Using New Words

Work alone or with a partner. Choose five target words and phrases from the list on page 106. On a piece of paper, use each word or phrase in a sentence.

Writing

Write a paragraph about a person you know. Begin your paragraph:

I think _____ *has . . . (a heart of gold / a big head / a big*
(name)

mouth / eyes in the back of his or her head). **Then give your reasons**

for saying this about the person.

REVIEWING VOCABULARY

A Write these words in the chart below: *adult*, *brain*, *elbow*, *heart*, *knee*, *nurse*, *patient*, *shoulder*, *sight*, *taste*, and *touch*.

Parts of the Body	
People	
Senses	

B Complete these sentences with the phrases in the box.

and so on	doesn't matter	figure out		made up	used to
can't stand	doesn't mind	in the middle of	take care of		

1. My new job will start at 7:00 in the morning. I'll have to get
   _____ getting up early.
2. I _____ green vegetables. No green beans or broccoli or
   spinach for me!
3. My father sometimes falls asleep _____ a movie.
4. Anna is going to the beach for the weekend. Who will
   _____ her cat?
5. There was a bad car accident. The police are trying to
   _____ why it happened.
6. We can use Dan's car. It's OK with him. He _____.
7. Do you want to go to the 7:00 or the 9:00 movie? It
   _____ to me.

8. The soccer team is _____ of twenty-four players.

9. Should I get all the usual things at the supermarket? Bread, milk, bananas, _____?

C Match the words below with their definitions. There are two extra words in the box.

consider	fix	mention	receive	special	support
emergency	human	perhaps	secret	store	trust

1. _____ = put something away to use later

2. _____ = repair something that isn't working

3. _____ = hold something up so it doesn't fall

4. _____ = get something that is given to you

5. _____ = think about something (before you decide)

6. _____ = belonging to or relating to people

7. _____ = better or more important than the usual

8. _____ = believe that someone is honest and will not hurt you

9. _____ = a plan or idea you don't tell other people about

10. _____ = speak or write about someone or something in a few words

EXPANDING VOCABULARY

Prefixes

A **prefix** added to the beginning of a word changes its meaning. For example, the prefix *un-* means "not." So *unhappy* means "not happy."

Add the prefix *un-* to each of the adjectives in the box. Complete the sentences with the new words.

clear	healthy	✔important	kind	lucky	usual

1. Don't worry about the distance. It doesn't matter. It's completely ___unimportant___.
2. There are some _____ types of animals in the Galápagos. They're very special.
3. She looks _____. Is she eating well? Does she get enough sleep?
4. That was not a nice thing to say to her. Don't be so _____!
5. The number 13 makes some people nervous. They think it's

   _____.
6. I don't understand his plan. It's _____ what he's going to do.

A PUZZLE

Complete the sentences with words you studied in Chapters 9–12. Write the words in the puzzle.

Across

1. Should she accept the new job? It's a difficult d_____.
5. He needs some a_____ about what classes to take.
6. It's not too difficult, but it's not simple, e_____.
7. You can't see well t_____ a dirty window.
9. It's early, but the students are a_____ in class.

Down

1. Children d_____ on their parents.
2. The teacher will not a_____ papers written in pencil.
3. It's raining. Do you s_____ want to go out?
4. There's no coffee. Will you have tea i_____?
5. The dry weather will a_____ the farmers in a bad way.
8. Keep trying! There's no r_____ to give up.

BUILDING DICTIONARY SKILLS

 A   **Look at the dictionary entries below.**

> pa•tient¹ /ˈpeɪʃənt/ *adj* able to deal with a problem or wait for something without getting angry or upset: *Try to be patient* **with** *the children.* ➤ ➤ opposite IMPATIENT
>
> pa•tient² *n* someone who is getting medical treatment: *There are 150 patients in the hospital.*

Do you see **patient¹** and **patient²**? The small, raised numbers are superscripts. They tell you that the two words are different.

Complete these sentences.

1. *Patient* can be ____an adjective____. It means _____
_____ .

2. *Patient* can also be _____ . It means _____ .
_____

B   **Sometimes there is no superscript, but there is more than one meaning for a word. The meanings are numbered. Look at the dictionary entries below.**

> heart /hɑrt/ *n* **1** the part of your body in your chest that pumps blood around your body **2** the part of you that feels strong emotions: *I know in my heart that I love her.* **3** a shape like a heart representing love

> sight /saɪt/ *n* **1** [U] the ability to see: *My grandmother is losing her sight.* **2** [U] when you see something: *I can't stand the sight of blood.* **3** something that is interesting to see because it is beautiful, large, unusual etc.: *The Space Needle is one of the most famous sights in Seattle.*

1. Circle *heart* in each sentence, and find its definition. Write the number of the meaning.

   a. __3__ She spells her name *K-e-l-l-i*, and writes it with a little heart above the *i*.

   b. ____ I'm afraid she's going to break his heart.

   c. ____ What kinds of exercise are best for your heart?

2. Circle *sight* in each sentence, and find its definition. Write the number of the meaning.

   a. ____ I want to visit London and see all the sights.

   b. ____ *Sight* and *eyesight* have the same meaning.

   c. ____ He smiled at the sight of his children playing in the snow.

UNIT
4

CAREER
PATHS

CHAPTER 13

Singing for Iraq

Shada Hassoun, winner of Star Academy

GETTING READY TO READ

Talk in a small group or with the class.

1. What do you see in the photo?

2. There are many talent shows on TV today. A talent show has people who are good at something like singing or dancing. People who watch the show vote for their favorite performer. What shows like this do you know of?

3. Is being a singer a good kind of job to have? Why or why not?

4. What do you know about Iraq?

READING

Look at the words next to the reading. Then read without stopping. Don't worry about new words. Don't stop to use a dictionary. Just keep reading!

Singing for Iraq

1   One Friday night some time ago, thousands[1] of Iraqis came together around their TVs. They tried not to listen to the **sounds** of fighting in the streets. They tried, just for a while, to forget all the **trouble** in their country. Instead, they focused their attention on[2] a **pretty** young singer. All eyes were on Shada Hassoun.

2   Shada was twenty-five years old, the daughter of an Iraqi father and a Moroccan mother. She **was born** and **grew up** in Morocco, and she went to school there and in France. She knew Iraq only from family stories and from TV.

3   It was because of TV that people in Iraq found out about Shada. She was on a talent show in Lebanon called *Star Academy*. She won Iraqi hearts by singing the much-loved song "Baghdad." It describes the Iraqi capital as a great and beautiful city. The words bring to mind Baghdad's long history. After Shada sang the song, newspapers across Iraq put her picture on the front page.

4   For four months, people **throughout** the Arab world watched the competition[3] on *Star Academy*. **Finally**, it was the last night of the show. Shada was now one of only four singers. She needed people to watch the show and vote for her by phone. However, at that time, watching TV and making phone calls were not simple things in Iraq. Because of the war, many people had no TV. Some had TVs but no **electricity**. Others had no phones.

5   One Iraqi town, Irbil, was quiet. There, it was safe to go outside. So in Irbil, thousands of people watched the show outside on a big screen.[4] They waited together for the results of the voting. Hours passed. Finally, after **midnight**, everyone

(continued)

[1] *thousands* = many times 1,000

[2] *focus their attention on* = think only about

[3] *competition* = a test of who is the best at something

[4] *screen* = a large flat white surface for showing a film

heard the **news**: Shada was the winner, thanks to more than 7 million phone calls from Iraq. There were **celebrations** in the streets of Irbil and in private homes throughout Iraq.

6   Shada's win **marked** the start of her **career** as a singer. A few months later, she visited Iraq for the first time. She wanted to say thank you. Many people thanked her, too. For a while, she took their minds off the war. Shada said, "I can feel them, like, really happy and they're smiling, especially in that **situation** they live in, and that's—I mean, it was my **dream**, to make them happy."

Shada's words come from a CNN Newsroom transcript retrieved January 25, 2009, from http://transcripts.cnn.com/TRANSCRIPTS/0703/31/cnr.02.html.

Quick Comprehension Check

Read these sentences about the reading. Circle T (true) or F (false).

1. Shada Hassoun is a singer.   T   F

2. She lives in Iraq.   T   F

3. She became famous on a TV talent show.   T   F

4. This happened during a bad time in Iraq.   T   F

5. People in Iraq cared a lot about Shada.   T   F

EXPLORING VOCABULARY

Thinking about the Target Vocabulary

 Find the words and phrases in bold in "Singing for Iraq" on pages 119 and 120. Write them in the list in alphabetical order.

1. career	6.	11.
2. celebrations	7.	12.
3.	8.	13.
4.	9.	14.
5.	10.	15.

B Which words and phrases are new to you? Circle them in the list on page 120. Then find them in the reading. Look at the context. Can you guess the meaning?

Using the Target Vocabulary

 A These sentences are **about the reading**. Complete them with the words and phrase in the box.

career	finally	marked	pretty	sounds
electricity	grow up	news	situation	

1. Shada Hassoun is nice to look at. She is a _____ young woman.

2. There was fighting in the streets of Iraqi cities. People inside their homes could hear the _____ of the fighting.

3. From the time Shada was born, all through her years as a child, she lived in Morocco. She didn't _____ in Iraq.

4. People waited a long time for the results of the *Star Academy* competition. _____, the show came to its last night.

5. We depend on _____ for the lights inside buildings and to make computers, TVs, and radios work.

6. Information about something that happened only a little while ago is called _____.

7. Shada's win on *Star Academy* _____ the beginning of big changes in her life. It showed when and where they all started.

8. Shada wanted a _____ as a singer. She wanted to do this as her life's work.

9. Shada was talking about everything happening in Iraq and affecting the Iraqi people when she mentioned the "_____ they live in."

B These sentences use the target words and phrase **in new contexts.** Complete them with the words and phrase in the box.

career	finally	marks	news	sound
electricity	grew up	pretty	situation	

1. You need to be careful with _____. It can be dangerous.

2. Watch the _____ on TV to find out what is happening in the world.

3. Gabriel was born in Puerto Rico, but he _____ in New York.

4. The TV isn't working. The picture is fine, but we can't hear any _____.

5. I tried and tried to call you, but _____, I gave up.

6. After Liz completed her education, she began her _____ as a nurse.

7. This year _____ the company's thirtieth year in business.

8. There were too many patients in the emergency room. It was a bad _____.

9. This strawberry ice cream cake tastes great, and it's _____ to look at, too.

C Read each **definition** and look at the paragraph number. Look back at the reading to find the right target word or phrase. Complete the chart.

Definition	Paragraph	Target Word or Phrase
1. problems that make something difficult	1	
2. came out of her mother's body	2	
3. in every part of something	4	
4. 12:00 at night	5	
5. parties because something good happened	5	
6. something nice you hope to do	6	

Word Grammar: Verbs in the Simple Past Tense

Form the simple past tense of **regular verbs** by adding -*(e)d* to the base form of the verb. The verbs *work* and *smile* are regular, so their past tense forms are *worked* and *smiled*.

Irregular verbs do not follow this rule. For example, the simple past tense forms of *eat* and *drink* are *ate* and *drank*.

In Chapter 13, you have seen the irregular simple past tense verbs *came*, *found out*, *heard*, *knew*, *put*, *sang*, *took*, *was*, *went*, *were*, and *won*. Write them after their base forms in the chart.

Irregular Verbs			
Base Form	Simple Past Tense Form	Base Form	Simple Past Tense Form
1. be	was or were	6. know	_____
2. come	_____	7. put	_____
3. find out	_____	8. sing	_____
4. go	_____	9. take	_____
5. hear	_____	10. win	_____

DEVELOPING YOUR SKILLS

Scanning

Read these questions about "Singing for Iraq." Scan the reading, and write short answers.

1. Where was Shada Hassoun born? _____
2. Where were her parents from? _____
3. What was *Star Academy*? _____
4. For how many months did the show go on? _____
5. What special song did Shada sing on the show? _____

6. What did Iraqi newspapers do? _____

7. On the last night of the show, how many phone calls did people in Iraq make to vote for Shada? _____

8. What happened when people heard the results of the voting?

_____

Summarizing

A   **These seven sentences make up a summary of the reading. Number the sentences in order.**

_____ **a.** She grew up in Morocco and never visited Iraq.

__1__ **b.** Shada Hassoun became important to many Iraqis during a time of great trouble.

_____ **c.** She then began her singing career and made her first visit to Iraq.

_____ **d.** At age twenty-five, she sang on *Star Academy*, a TV talent show.

_____ **e.** Shada was born to an Iraqi father and a Moroccan mother.

_____ **f.** Votes from Iraq made Shada the winner.

_____ **g.** The show was watched throughout the Arab world.

B   **Write the sentences in Part A as a paragraph.**

_____

_____

_____

_____

_____

_____

_____

_____

Discussion

Talk about these questions in a small group or with the class.

1. What was the situation in Iraq at the time when Shada won *Star Academy*?

2. Why do you think Shada became so important to people in Iraq?

3. There are many reasons why someone may win a talent show. What do you think matters most in the end?

   a. the person's talent or skill   **c.** luck

   b. what he or she looks like   **d.** other: _____

Using New Words

Work alone or with a partner. Choose five of the target words or phrases from the list on page 120. On a piece of paper, use each word or phrase in a sentence.

Writing

Write a short paragraph about yourself. Tell where you were born and where you grew up. Tell something about your family and your education.

CHAPTER 14

From Play to Work

*Murat Sanal beside the
Bosporus in Istanbul*

GETTING READY TO READ

Talk about these questions with a partner.

1. The man in the photo is from Istanbul. Where is this city?

2. Adults sometimes ask children, "What do you want to be when you grow up?" How did you answer that question? Complete this statement:

   When I was _____ years old, I wanted to be a/an _____.

   Give your reasons.

READING

Look at the words and pictures next to the reading. Then read without stopping.

From Play to Work

1   When you were a child, did you **ever** play with Legos?[1] Murat Sanal did. He loved building all kinds of things from those little plastic pieces. Today, he is an architect.[2] He says, "It all began with Legos."

2   Murat grew up in Istanbul, the capital of Turkey. He studied architecture at a university there. Then he went to another university in the United States. **At first**, he took courses in English as a Second Language (ESL). In the ESL **program**, he met interesting people from all over the world. Later, he went on with his studies in architecture.

3   After **graduation**, Murat got his first job as an architect. He worked at a ski resort[3] in Vail, Colorado, in the United States. He went there with two friends from Istanbul. All three of them loved to ski.[4] "It was a great place to work," he says. In Vail, they could go skiing even during lunch hour. They were **serious** about their jobs, but they had a lot of fun, too.

4   Now Murat is back home in Turkey. He lives in Istanbul, near the Bosporus.[5] He walks **along** the water to **get to** work. His office is only ten minutes **away**, and he likes that. His job is with an architecture company. The company works on many different types of **projects**: houses, apartment buildings, resorts, and so on. Murat likes the **variety** of projects. He likes the people at the company, too.

5   Murat does not have a **regular** work **schedule**. It changes from day to day, but he does not mind. Murat usually works long hours[6]—often ten hours a day, sometimes more than fifty hours a week. His schedule depends on his projects. They often leave him little time to **relax**. He says, "In this **profession**, there are lots of hours."

(continued)

[1] *Legos*

[2] an *architect* = a person who draws and plans buildings

[3] a *resort* = a place with many hotels, often at the beach or in the mountains

[4] He's *skiing*.

[5] the *Bosporus* = the narrow waterway between the Black Sea and the Sea of Marmara

[6] *long hours* = work days that are longer than usual

6   Murat likes variety in his work. He cannot stand doing the same things again and again. He says, "In my job, every project is a new start. It's great exercise for the mind." Murat is **proud** of his work. He is making better places for people to live and work and play.

Quick Comprehension Check

Read these sentences about the reading. Circle T (true) or F (false).

1. Murat Sanal learned to play with Legos at a university in Turkey.   T   F

2. He studied architecture, and today he is an architect.   T   F

3. His first job as an architect was in Turkey.   T   F

4. Now he lives and works in Istanbul.   T   F

5. Murat says that architects work long hours.   T   F

6. He is unhappy at his job.   T   F

EXPLORING VOCABULARY

Thinking about the Target Vocabulary

 Find the words and phrases in bold in "From Play to Work" on pages 127 and 128. Write them in the list in alphabetical order.

1. along	6.	11.
2. at first	7.	12.
3.	8.	13.
4.	9.	14.
5.	10.	15.

 Which words and phrases are new to you? Circle them here. Then find them in the reading. Look at the context. Can you guess the meaning?

Using the Target Vocabulary

A These sentences are **about the reading**. What is the meaning of each **boldfaced** word or phrase? Circle a, b, or c.

1. When you were a child, did you **ever** play with Legos? Murat did. *Ever* means
   a. at any time. **b.** either. **c.** instead.

2. Murat went to the United States to study. **At first**, he studied ESL. *At first* means
   a. at best. **b.** luckily. **c.** in the beginning.

3. He studied in an ESL **program** at a U.S. university. In this sentence, *program* means
   a. a type of company. **b.** a special group of courses. **c.** a government office.

4. Murat had fun in Vail, but he was **serious** about his job. *Serious* means
   a. being crazy. **b.** feeling sleepy. **c.** thinking carefully.

5. It takes Murat only ten minutes to **get to** his office from his home. *Get to* means
   a. arrive at. **b.** receive. **c.** figure out.

6. Murat's office is only ten minutes **away** from his house. *Away* means
   a. at a distance. **b.** high or tall. **c.** anywhere.

7. Murat likes working on a **variety** of projects. *A variety of projects* means the projects are
   a. all the same. **b.** different. **c.** quick and easy.

8. Murat doesn't work **regular** hours. His hours are always changing. In this sentence, *regular* means
   a. good enough. **b.** a lot of, many. **c.** always happening at the same times.

9. Murat works long hours, with little time to **relax**. *Relax* means

   a. stop worrying and enjoy life.　**b.** do dangerous things.　**c.** be in a relationship.

10. Murat is making better places for people to live. That makes him **proud**. *Proud* means feeling

   a. happy about a good thing you did.　**b.** sorry about a mistake you made.　**c.** nervous about your future.

B These sentences use the target words and phrases **in new contexts**. Complete them with the words and phrases in the box.

at first	ever	program	regular	serious
away	get to	proud	relax	variety

1. Most college students in the United States live _____ from home.

2. You can see a great _____ of shows on TV.

3. I sometimes forget people's names. Do you _____ do that?

4. It takes me about half an hour to _____ school in the morning.

5. Luisa is going to finish college and then begin a _____ in Business Administration.

6. _____, their relationship was a secret. After a while, people found out.

7. I start and finish work at the same time every day. I'm used to working _____ hours.

8. Dr. Patel talks about his children all the time. He's very _____ of them.

9. We'll take care of everything. Don't worry. You can _____.

10. Please be _____. This situation is nothing to laugh about.

Read each definition and look at the paragraph number. Look back at the reading to find the right target word. Complete the chart.

Definition	Paragraph	Target Word
1. the time when a person finishes high school or college	3	
2. by the side of something, from one part of it to another	4	
3. pieces of work that take time and planning	4	
4. a plan of when things are going to happen	5	
5. work that people need a special type of education to do	5	

Word Grammar: *Graduation* and Its Word Family

When you learn a new word, try to learn other words in the same word family. For example, the words *graduation*, *grad*, and *graduate* are all in the same word family.

 These sentences use *graduation* or another word in the same word family. Underline the word, and write *noun*, *verb*, or *adjective*.

1. Most U.S. high school students <u>graduate</u> in June.
   <u>   verb   </u>

2. She's a graduate of Harvard Law School.
   <u>   </u>

3. Graduation will be on June 2.
   <u>   </u>

4. After college, he's going to grad school.
   <u>   </u>

5. They're graduate students at NYU.
   <u>   </u>

B Complete the chart with the words from Part A.

Nouns	Verbs	Adjectives
	graduate	

DEVELOPING YOUR SKILLS

Pronoun Reference

What do the boldfaced pronouns mean in these sentences? Look back at the reading. Write the answers.

1. Paragraph 1: Today, **he** is an architect. Murat
2. Paragraph 3: All three of **them** loved to ski. _____
3. Paragraph 3: "**It** was a great place to work." _____
4. Paragraph 5: **It** changes from day to day. _____
5. Paragraph 5: **They** often leave him little time to relax. _____

Understanding Sentences with *Because*

A **Choose the best way to complete each sentence. Write the letters.**

____ 1. Murat played with Legos

____ 2. He studied architecture in college

____ 3. Murat likes variety in his work

____ 4. His company gives him a lot of variety

____ 5. His schedule often changes

____ 6. Murat is proud of his work

a. because he wanted to be an architect.

b. because it does many different types of projects.

c. because he loved building things with them.

d. because it depends on the work he's doing.

e. because he's making better places for people to live, work, and play.

f. because he can't stand doing the same thing all the time.

B **Complete this sentence. Then compare answers with a partner.**

I (like / don't like) variety in my (work / classes / everyday life / food /_____) because _____

_____.

Summarizing

A These seven sentences make up a summary of the reading. Number the sentences in order.

_____ **a.** Then he went on with his studies in the United States.

_____ **b.** At school in Turkey, he studied architecture.

_____ **c.** The company does many different types of projects.

__1__ **d.** As a child, Murat Sanal loved building things with Legos.

_____ **e.** Murat feels proud of his work on these projects.

_____ **f.** After graduation, he worked as an architect at a ski resort.

_____ **g.** Now he works for a company in Istanbul.

B Write the sentences in Part A as a paragraph.

_____

_____

_____

_____

_____

_____

_____

Discussion

Talk about these questions in a small group.

1. What are three things Murat likes about his job?

2. How many hours a week do you consider "full-time work"?

3. How does Murat feel about his long hours at work? How would you feel about so many hours?

4. How many weeks of vacation time should a worker have in a year? Does your answer depend on the worker's type of job? Does it depend on the number of years on the job?

5. How many hours a week should full-time students spend on school work?

Using New Words

Ask and answer the questions with a partner. Then talk about your answers with the class.

1. Do you go to bed and get up at **regular** times, or is your **schedule** different every day?

2. How long does it take you to **get to** school?

3. What is something you are **serious** about?

4. Who or what do you feel **proud** of? Who is proud of you?

5. What do you do to **relax**?

Writing

What matters most to you in a job? Check (✓) your answers. Think about why these things matter.

☐ good pay   ☐ a variety of things to do   ☐ a regular schedule
☐ nice people   ☐ a good location (place)   ☐ other: _____

Write a paragraph about your idea of a good job. You can begin: *A good job is a job with . . .*

Listening for the Truth

*The Honorable
Judith Prakash*

GETTING READY TO READ

Talk about these questions in a small group or with the whole class.

1. Judith Prakash is a judge. What do judges do? Describe their work.
2. Is being a judge a good job? Why or why not?

Look at the words and picture next to the reading. Then read without stopping.

Listening for the Truth

1   Judith Prakash is a **judge** in Singapore. She is a judge on the Supreme Court. It is the highest **court** in the country. Being a judge is a serious job. It is a job with a lot of **responsibility**. Judges make important decisions. Their decisions can change people's lives.

2   A big part of Judge Prakash's job is listening. In court, she listens and learns about **disagreements** between people. The people come to court with their **lawyers**, and the lawyers speak about the case.[1] Judge Prakash was a lawyer herself for many years. The lawyers **argue** about the facts of each case. Sometimes they argue about the meaning of a **law**. Other people speak in court, too. Everyone **promises** to **tell the truth**.

3   "Every case is different, so they're all interesting to me," says Judge Prakash. She asks many questions in court. The cases give her a lot to think about. She likes this, but making a decision is never easy. She has to ask herself, "Do I have the whole story,[2] or do I need to know more?" Another important question is: Who is telling the truth? She has to figure that out. She says, "That's the hardest part of my job."

4   Things are changing in Singapore. For many years, there were no women on the Supreme Court there. All the judges were men. Right now, there are only three women **among** the fourteen judges. However, in the lower courts,[3] almost half the judges are women. These younger women can look at Judge Prakash as a role model.[4] They can **follow** her example. She did not really have any role models to follow, but she felt **confident** about becoming a judge. She says, "I never **doubted** myself. I knew I had the **ability** to do the job."

[1] a *case* = a disagreement that must be decided in court

[2] *the whole story* = all the information about something

[3] the *lower courts* = courts below the Supreme Court

[4] a *role model* = someone who other people want to be like

5   In court, people speak to Judge Prakash with great respect. When she **enters** the courtroom, everyone stops talking. They all stand up. People bow[5] to her. They call her "Your Honor" to show their respect. They always listen carefully to her. It is very different at home, she says. "I have four daughters, and they never listen!"

[5] He's *bowing.*

Quick Comprehension Check

Read these sentences about the reading. Circle T (true) or F (false).

1. Judith Prakash is a judge in Singapore.   T   F

2. Lawyers listen to disagreements between judges.   T   F

3. Making decisions in court is easy for Judge Prakash.   T   F

4. She says, "Everyone tells the truth in court."   T   F

5. She was nervous about becoming a judge.   T   F

6. In court, people listen carefully to Judge Prakash.   T   F

EXPLORING VOCABULARY

Thinking about the Target Vocabulary

A   Find the words and phrases in **bold** in "Listening for the Truth" on page 136. Write them in the list in alphabetical order.

1. ability	6.	11.
2. among	7.	12.
3.	8.	13.
4.	9.	14.
5.	10.	15.

B   **Which words and phrases are new to you? Circle them here. Then find them in the reading. Look at the context. Can you guess the meaning?**

Using the Target Vocabulary

 These sentences are about the reading. Complete them with the words in the box.

ability	argue	doubt	follow	promise
among	confident	enters	judge	responsibility

1. Judith Prakash is a _____. She makes decisions in court cases.

2. Judges do an important job. People depend on them. Their decisions can affect many lives. A judge has a job with a lot of _____.

3. A judge listens to the lawyers for both sides. The lawyers don't agree. They _____ about the facts of a case.

4. Everyone in court says, "I will tell the truth." They _____ to tell the truth.

5. Judge Prakash is one of a group of judges. There are only three women _____ the fourteen judges.

6. Years ago, there were no women judges in Singapore. So, as a child, Judith couldn't say, "I want to be like *her.*" She could not _____ the example of other women.

7. Judith Prakash knew she could be a good judge. She was not nervous. She felt _____.

8. She was sure that she could do the job. She did not _____ her _____ to do it.

9. People stand up when a judge _____ (comes into) the courtroom.

B These sentences use the target words **in new contexts**. Complete them with the words in the box.

ability	argue	doubted	follow	promised
among	confident	enter	judges	responsibility

1. I am _____ that you will pass the test.

2. You can't go in there. It says "Do Not _____" on the door.

3. The teacher said, "Do Exercise A for homework. Read the directions and _____ the examples."

4. Ann's son didn't always tell the truth, but she always believed him. She never _____ him.

5. Your sense of sight is your _____ to see.

6. There's great interest in this new program _____ students at the university.

7. Maria's husband hates to _____ with her, so he just says, "OK, fine, anything you want."

8. My friend asked me to call her and I _____ to do that.

9. Which film is the best? The _____ will decide on the winner.

10. They wanted to make him the president, but he didn't want so much

    _____.

C Read these sentences. Match the **boldfaced** target words and phrase with their definitions.

a. Many reporters and photographers waited outside the **court**.

b. The police stopped the driver. He broke the **law** by driving too fast.

c. Some people never **tell the truth**.

d. She asked her **lawyer** for advice about selling her farm.

e. Do you know the reason for their **disagreement**?

Target Words and Phrase	Definitions
1. _____	= give the real facts about something
2. _____	= a room where a judge listens to information about a case
3. _____	= a rule made by a government to say what people can or cannot do
4. _____	= someone who gives advice about laws or speaks for people in court
5. _____	= an argument, or a situation where people have different opinions

Word Grammar: *Disagreement* and Its Word Family

When you learn a new word, it's a good idea to learn other words in the same word family. Study the words related to *disagreement* in the chart below.

Nouns	Verbs	Adjectives
agreement	agree	agreeable
disagreement	disagree	disagreeable

Use words from the chart to complete these sentences.

1. They want to paint the kitchen, but they can't _____ on a color.
2. We're lucky to have this _____ weather.
3. The lawyers finally came to an _____.
4. One brother wants to spend the money, but the others _____.
5. He's very _____ in the morning when he doesn't get enough sleep.
6. The trouble started with a _____ over a piece of land.

DEVELOPING YOUR SKILLS

Topics of Paragraphs

A Look at the list of paragraph topics from "Listening for the Truth."
Find the paragraph on each topic in the reading. Write the paragraph
number (1–5).

a. what happens in court   Paragraph ____

b. changes in Singapore   Paragraph ____

c. who Judith Prakash is   Paragraph ____

d. her courtroom versus her home   Paragraph ____

e. what Judge Prakash says about her job   Paragraph ____

B Write a sentence about each of the six topics from paragraphs 1–5. Use
information from the reading.

1. _____

2. _____

3. _____

4. _____

5. _____

Summarizing

Use information from the reading to complete this summary.

Judith Prakash is a _____ in Singapore. She has
                              (1)

a job with a lot of _____. Judge Prakash has to listen to
                           (2)

_____ between people. She has to figure out who is telling
        (3)

the _____. Then she has to make a _____.
          (4)   (5)

In _____, people listen to her and speak to her with great
        (6)

_____. At home, she says, things are different!
        (7)

Discussion

Talk about these questions in a small group.

1. What is the hardest part of Judge Prakash's job? Why do you think this is?

2. What does the reading say has changed in Singapore? Why do you think this change has happened?

3. How do you show respect to a person? To whom do you show respect? Why do you show them respect?

Using New Words

Work with a partner. Take turns completing these statements. Then tell the class something about your partner.

1. I sometimes **argue** with _____.We **argue** about . . .

2. I **followed** _____'s example when I . . .

3. I (feel / don't feel) **confident** when I . . .

4. I (always / usually / rarely / never) **tell the truth** when . . .

Writing

Some people want a job with a lot of responsibility. Some people don't. What about you? Write a paragraph about your feelings. You can begin: *I (would like / wouldn't like) a job with a lot of responsibility because . . .*

CHAPTER 16 Trying to Understand

Gil Conchas in his office

GETTING READY TO READ

Talk about these questions with your class.

1. The man in the photo teaches at a university. Is that a good job? Tell why or why not.

2. What can you study at a university? Make a list of subjects: *English, history, law, architecture, . . .*

3. You will be reading about Gil and about his brother. Who in the class has brothers? Who has sisters? Is anyone in the class an only child?[1]

[1] *an only child* = a person with no brothers or sisters

READING

Look at the words and picture next to the reading. Then read.

Trying to Understand

1   Gil Conchas is a professor[1] at the University of California. He teaches courses in education and sociology.[2] Like most professors, he also does **research**. Gil studies large groups of people. He studies the things they believe and the things they say and do. Doing research means he never stops learning.

2   Growing up, Gil did not know much about universities or research. His family was very poor. He was born in California, but his parents were from Mexico. They did not speak English well. They worked on farms and picked grapes, tomatoes, and strawberries.[3] They also worked in **factories**. Gil's parents had a hard life, and he did not want that for himself.

3   At age five, Gil was already a great help to his parents. He spoke English well, and he was their interpreter.[4] One time, his mother had to take a case to court, and Gil went with her. He loved helping his mother. Other **relatives** depended on him, too. "Where's Gil? We need Gil!" they said. It made him feel grown-up.[5]

4   Gil was a **smart** and hard-working student, so he got good **grades**. Because of his **success** in school, he had the **chance** to go to a very good university. He did well there, too, and could choose any profession he wanted.

5   Now Gil does research on poor boys and girls in the United States, especially **ones** who live in cities. Many of these children live in difficult and even dangerous situations. Some of them—like Gil—grow up and find success as adults. Others do not. Why do some **succeed** and others **fail**? What should the government do? How can other people help? Gil is working to find answers to these questions. He **explains** his research in his first book, *The Color of Success*, and in his second, *Small Schools and Urban Youth*.[6]

[1] a *professor* = a teacher at a college or university

[2] *sociology* = the study of how people act in large social groups

[3] *grapes*, *tomatoes*, and a *strawberry*

[4] an *interpreter* = a person who listens to a speaker and repeats his or her words in another language

[5] *grown-up* = adult

[6] *urban youth* = young people in cities

6   Gil is also writing a book about his brother Jesse. Jesse is in **prison**. He was in a fight on the street. There was a **crowd** of about twenty young men, and one of them died. In prison, Jesse graduated from high school and is taking college courses. Gil calls or writes to him every day, and he thinks about him often. He **compares** his brother's life with his own and **wonders**, "What made our lives so different?"

7   Gil's success makes his parents very proud. However, they do not really understand his work. Gil's father told him, "All I know is, you're doing good for other people—that's what makes me happy." Gil now lives and works in a world that is very different from his parents'. "But," he says, "any time I can, I go home for comfort."[7]

[7] *comfort* = a feeling of being relaxed and happy

Quick Comprehension Check

Read these sentences about the reading. Circle T (true) or F (false).

1. Gil Conchas is a student at the University of California.   T   F

2. His parents worked on farms and in factories.   T   F

3. Gil wanted to do the same type of work as his parents.   T   F

4. Today, he studies the lives of poor boys and girls in U.S. cities.   T   F

5. He's also writing a book about his life.   T   F

6. Gil is close to his family.   T   F

EXPLORING VOCABULARY

Thinking about the Vocabulary

A Find the words in **bold** in "Trying to Understand" on pages 144 and 145. Write them in the list in alphabetical order.

1. *chance*	6.	11.
2. *compares*	7.	12.
3.	8.	13.
4.	9.	14.
5.	10.	15.

B Which words are new to you? Circle them here. Then find them in the reading. Look at the context. Can you guess the meaning?

Using the Target Vocabulary

A These sentences are **about the reading**. What is the meaning of each **boldfaced** word or phrase? Circle a, b, or c.

1. Gil Conchas **does research** and writes about what he learns. *Do research* means

   a. spend time talking. **b.** read students' papers. **c.** look for new facts.

2. He helped his parents and other **relatives**, too. Your relatives are

   a. people in your family. **b.** your friends. **c.** people at your job.

3. Gil was **smart** and a hard worker, so he did well in school. *Smart* means

   a. crazy but lucky. **b.** shy and nervous. **c.** good at learning.

4. Gil worked hard and had great **success** in school. *Success* means

   a. a good end to what you tried to do. **b.** a variety of problems. **c.** projects and other things to do.

5. Gil **succeeded in** building a different kind of life for himself. *Succeeded in* means

   a. had trouble with.   **b.** did very well in.   **c.** only dreamed about.

6. Many boys aren't like Gil. They **fail** to make good lives for themselves. *Fail to do something* means

   a. have fun doing it.   **b.** try to, but not do it.   **c.** be good at doing it.

7. In the books he writes, Gil **explains** his research and what he finds out. *Explain something* means

   a. make it easy to understand.   **b.** receive or accept it.   **c.** cannot stand it.

8. Gil's brother was part of a **crowd** that had a fight in the street. A crowd is

   a. a product or result.   **b.** a project.   **c.** a large group of people.

9. Gil **wonders**, "What made our lives so different?" *He wonders* means

   a. he argues.   **b.** he describes.   **c.** he asks himself.

B These sentences use the target words **in new contexts**. Complete them with the words in the box.

crowd	fail	research	succeeded	wonder
explain	relatives	smart	success	

1. Ask the teacher to _____ what the word means.

2. A _____ waited outside the court to hear the news.

3. People respect Hillary's ideas. They say she is very _____.

4. On my grandfather's birthday, most of my _____ came to dinner at our house.

5. That history course is hard, but Ayako's a good student. She won't _____.

6. These scientists are going to Antarctica to do _____.

7. I start my new job Monday. I _____ what it will be like.

8. On their next try, they _____ in climbing the mountain.

9. She's having great _____ in her acting career. She's working on her fifth movie.

Read these sentences. Match the boldfaced target words with their definitions.

a. The professor said, "In your paper, describe the movie and **compare** it with the book."

b. I promised to call her back, but then I didn't get a **chance** to do it.

c. The judge said, "You will spend the next ten years in **prison**."

d. When Gil was a student, he got good **grades** on tests and papers.

e. **Factory** workers usually have regular work schedules.

f. These glasses are out of style. I want some new **ones**.

Target Words	Definitions
1. _____	= a time or a situation when you can do something
2. _____	= a place where people have to stay when they break the law
3. _____	= a place where people use machines to make products
4. _____	= look at how people or things are the same or different
5. _____	= letters or numbers that tell how well someone did in school
6. _____	= a pronoun meaning someone or something already mentioned (here, *glasses*)

Word Grammar: *One* and *Ones*

The word *one* can be a pronoun. Remember: Pronouns (such as *I*, *he*, *him*, *they*, *them*) take the place of nouns. We can use *one* and *ones* for people or things.

- *One* can take the place of *a/an* + a singular noun.

  one
  She has a car, but I don't have a̶ ̶c̶a̶r̶.

- *Ones* can take the place of a plural noun.

  ones
  These books are John's. The b̶o̶o̶k̶s̶ on the table are mine.

- *One* or *ones* can be used with an adjective.
  You have small ears. I have **big ones**.

- *Ones* is often used with *this* or *that*.
  I don't like that shirt, but **this one** is nice.

Look for a noun that is used twice. Change the second noun to *one* or *ones*.

one
1. He's reading a book. It's a very long b̶o̶o̶k̶.

2. Ms. Summers is an artist, and she's a very good artist.

3. Lora has an older brother and two younger brothers.

4. Make a list of products from your country. Which are the most important products?

5. That bag belongs to Steve, and this bag is Barbara's.

6. This weekend, there were several small car accidents and two really bad accidents.

7. Asia is the largest continent. The smallest continents are Australia and Europe.

DEVELOPING YOUR SKILLS

Pronoun Reference

What do the boldfaced pronouns mean in these sentences? Look back at the reading. Write the answers.

1. Paragraph 1: . . . **he** also does research. Gil_____
2. Paragraph 2: **They** did not speak English well. _____
3. Paragraph 3: . . . and Gil went with **her**. _____
4. Paragraph 3: Other relatives depended on **him**, too. _____
5. Paragraph 3: "We need Gil!," **they** said. _____
6. Paragraph 5: . . . especially **ones** who live in cities. _____
7. Paragraph 6: **He** was in a fight on the street. _____
8. Paragraph 7: "All **I** know is, you're doing good for . . ." _____

Sentences with *Because*

A **Complete the sentences. Use information from the reading.**

1. Growing up, Gil did not want a life like his parents' because _____
   _____.

2. Gil was a great help to his parents, even as a child, because _____
   _____.

3. Gil was able to go to a very good university because _____
   _____.

4. Gil goes back home when he can because _____
   _____.

B **Complete the sentences. Use your own ideas.**

1. Gil does research on poor boys and girls in the United States because
   _____.

2. Gil writes books about his research because _____
   _____.

Summarizing

A **These sentences make up a summary of the reading. Number the sentences in order.**

_____ **a.** Now he's teaching at a university and doing research.

_____ **b.** His parents were from Mexico, and his family was poor.

_____ **c.** It is about the lives of poor boys and girls in the United States.

_8_ **d.** Gil's whole family is important to him.

_1_ **e.** Gil Conchas was born in California.

_____ **f.** He also speaks and writes about his brother in prison.

_____ **g.** He helped them by speaking English for them.

_____ **h.** Gil always worked hard in school and did well.

B **Write the sentences from Part A as a paragraph.**

_____

_____

_____

_____

_____

_____

_____

_____

_____

_____

_____

_____

_____

_____

_____

_____

_____

_____

Sharing Opinions

What does success mean to you? Circle your answers to the questions below. Then talk with a partner. Find out what he or she thinks and why.

1 = Very important   3 = Not very important
2 = Important   4 = It doesn't matter

How important is . . .	Your Answers	Your Partner's Answers
1. being famous?	1 2 3 4	1 2 3 4
2. making a lot of money?	1 2 3 4	1 2 3 4
3. being free to do what you want?	1 2 3 4	1 2 3 4
4. being married and having children?	1 2 3 4	1 2 3 4
5. having a job with a lot of responsibility?	1 2 3 4	1 2 3 4
6. having the respect of other people?	1 2 3 4	1 2 3 4

Using New Words

Work with a partner. Choose five of the target words from the list on page 146. On a piece of paper, use each word in a sentence.

Writing

Write a paragraph comparing yourself to a brother or sister or another relative. Write about ways you are different or ways you are alike. You can begin: *My (older sister/mother/brother) and I are (very different/a lot alike)*. You can use sentences like:

My sister always _____, but I _____.

My father likes to _____, but I _____.

We both _____.

UNIT 4 Wrap-up

REVIEWING VOCABULARY

A Write words from the box in the correct part of the chart. There are two extra words.

ability court factory judge lawyer prison relative wonder

People	
Places	

B Match the words with their definitions. Write the letter.

____ **1.** a law

____ **2.** a crowd

____ **3.** the truth

____ **4.** a career

____ **5.** research

____ **6.** responsibility

____ **7.** trouble

____ **8.** variety

a. problems

b. the facts about something

c. careful study to find out new facts

d. a large group of people together in a place

e. something you have to take care of and be serious about

f. a profession or job that someone does for a long time

g. differences within something that make it interesting

h. a rule that all the people of a state or country have to follow

153

Complete these sentences with the words and phrases in the box. There are two extra words.

| at first | doubt | followed | grow up | smart | success |
| compares | failed | get to | situation | sound | throughout |

1. You're _____ , so I'm sure you'll figure it out.

2. The adults asked the children, "What do you want to do when you _____?"

3. How long does it take you to _____ school in the morning?

4. He always _____ his life here to his life back home.

5. _____, he didn't want to taste it, but then he tried it and liked it.

6. He _____ his brother's example and became a mountain climber.

7. She believes that she can keep her plan a secret, but I _____ it.

8. There were car accidents _____ the city because of the snow.

9. The test was very hard, and several students _____ it.

10. You need to know the history to understand the _____.

EXPANDING VOCABULARY

Suffixes

A **suffix** comes at the end of a word. It can tell you something about a word's meaning and use. For example, the suffixes -*ment* and -*tion* change verbs into nouns.

Use the nouns and verbs in the chart to complete the sentences.

Nouns	Verbs
argument	argue
agreement	agree
celebration	celebrate
explanation	explain
relaxation	relax

1. a. They're having another _____.
   b. Don't _____ with me!

2. a. Do you _____ with them?
   b. The two governments have an _____.

3. a. The _____ went on past midnight.
   b. We want to _____ your success!

4. a. Can you _____ what happened?
   b. I wonder what his _____ will be.

5. a. What do you do for _____?
   b. A hot shower helps me _____.

A PUZZLE

There are ten target words from Unit 4 in this puzzle. The words go across (→) and down (↓). Find the words and circle them. Use the words to complete the sentences below.

```
A   X   A   W   A   Y   Y   X   F   C
L   N   S   T   X   Z   D   Z   P   O
O   F   Z   D   W   E   V   E   R   N
N   H   P   W   H   X   Z   V   E   F
G   W   R   V   A   M   O   N   G   I
P   R   O   J   E   C   T   T   U   D
W   Q   U   B   H   R   X   V   L   E
Z   X   D   T   Q   N   J   X   A   N
F   P   R   O   M   I   S   E   R   T
Q   T   R   Z   C   H   A   N   C   E
```

Across

1. Please _____ me that you'll call me later!

2. We can walk to the library from here. It's only five minutes _____.

3. Do you _____ wonder what it's like to be rich and famous?

4. The boys are working on a _____ for their science class.

5. Are there good relationships _____ all the players on the team?

6. Shada finally had the _____ to meet her relatives in Iraq.

Down

7. We traveled east on the road _____ the river.

8. The patient's heartbeat was slow and _____.

9. Yuri wants to make his parents _____ of him.

10. I feel _____ that the program will be a success.

BUILDING DICTIONARY SKILLS

 A A word can have more than one meaning. It can also have more than one use. Look at these dictionary entries.

> **pro•gram**[1] /ˈproʊɡræm, -ɡrəm/ *n* **1** a set of instructions that a computer uses to do a particular job **2** a show on television or radio: *What's your favorite program?* **3** a printed description of what will happen at a play etc.: *Do you want to buy a program?* **4** a set of planned activities with a specific purpose
>
> **P** **pro•gram**[2] *v* (**programming, programmed**) to give a computer the instructions it needs to do a particular job

Now look at the uses of *program* in these sentences. Write *noun* or *verb* on the line followed by the number of the meaning.

1. He programs computers for the university.   <u>verb</u>   <u>—</u>

2. You can read the actors' names in the program.   <u> </u>   <u> </u>

3. There's a program about the Olympics on TV.   <u> </u>   <u> </u>

4. He's in a graduate program in business.   <u> </u>   <u> </u>

5. She writes programs for computer games.   <u> </u>   <u> </u>

 B Dictionaries sometimes show verb forms. Look at the entry for *program*[2].

• The *-ing* form of the verb is spelled *programming*.

• The simple past tense form is spelled *programmed*. Both verbs have a double *m*.

The verb *program* is regular; it ends in *-ed*. Dictionaries do not usually show the verb with *-ed*. There is no need to. However, dictionaries always show the simple past forms of irregular verbs.

> **tell** /tɛl/ *v* (*past* **told** /toʊld/) **1** to speak to someone and give facts or information about something: *Tell me what happened.* ➤ ➤ compare SAY[1] **2** to say that . . .

> **suc•ceed** /sək'sid/ *v* **1** to do well, to do what you tried to do: *If you try hard, you'll succeed.* ➤ ➤ compare FAIL **2** to have the result or effect something is . . .

1. Look at the entry for the verb *tell*.

    a. Is it a regular or an irregular verb?   _____

    b. What is the simple past tense form?   _____

2. Look at the entry for the word *succeed*.

    a. Is it a regular or an irregular verb?   _____

    b. What is the simple past tense form?   _____

Vocabulary Self-Test 2

Circle the letter of the word or phrase that best completes each sentence.

Example: The sun goes down in the _____.

    a. artist   **b.** race   **c.** west   **d.** result

1. It's cold, so it's hard to breathe _____ my nose.

    a. among   **b.** instead   **c.** through   **d.** away

2. We need to _____ the answer to this math problem.

    a. relax   **b.** figure out   **c.** mind   **d.** grow up

3. She had a bad car _____, but she's fine now.

    a. truth   **b.** sight   **c.** nurse   **d.** accident

4. The foreign students are new here and are not _____ the weather.

    a. used to   **b.** proud of   **c.** special to   **d.** kind to

5. It was easy to play the game. We just _____ the directions.

    a. followed   **b.** argued   **c.** supported   **d.** received

6. Some rich people have their own _____ planes.

    a. middle   **b.** confident   **c.** private   **d.** human

7. He doesn't care about clothes. Clothes don't _____ to him.

    a. matter   **b.** consider   **c.** mind   **d.** fail

8. She talked about two friends, but she didn't _____ their names.

    a. accept   **b.** mention   **c.** fix   **d.** wonder

9. An _____ is a group of words with a special meaning, like *put your foot in your mouth*.

    a. advice   **b.** elbow   **c.** adult   **d.** idiom

10. Who will _____ the baby when her parents are at work?

    a. store   **b.** depend on   **c.** take care of   **d.** taste

11. I can't explain it, but _____ someone else can.
    a. ever   b. perhaps   c. either   d. clear

12. The cars of the future may use _____ instead of gas.
    a. sound   b. electricity c. trouble   d. blood

13. _____, he felt nervous, but then he relaxed.
    a. And so on b. Along   c. One   d. At first

14. It's worth a lot of money because it's made of _____.
    a. law   b. success   c. profession   d. gold

15. Albert Einstein _____ in 1879 and died in 1955.
    a. made up   b. was born   c. trusted   d. considered

16. Look at the _____ to find out what time the next train is.
    a. shoulder   b. relative   c. schedule   d. responsibility

17. We waited for hours, and then _____, we heard the results.
    a. finally   b. already   c. salty   d. lucky

18. Her new job is a good _____ for her skills and interests.
    a. match   b. touch   c. crowd   d. secret

19. The judge has a professional _____ with each of the lawyers.
    a. graduation b. relationship c. variety   d. chance

20. Your hard work shows that you are _____ about your education.
    a. human   b. usual   c. serious   d. pretty

21. It is the _____ of many bird-watchers to visit the Galápagos.
    a. brain   b. dream   c. bone   d. type

22. My cold is affecting my _____ of smell.
    a. heart   b. prison   c. project   d. sense

23. It gets cold after dark, especially after _____.
    a. plastic   b. program   c. midnight   d. decision

24. My friend told me some surprising _____.
    a. news   b. metal   c. ability   d. emergency

25. The boy's parents want to talk to his teacher about his _____ in math and English.
    a. patients   b. factories   c. reasons   d. grades

26. Graduation from college _____ a new beginning for many people.

    a. can't stand   **b.** doubts   **c.** marks   **d.** enters

27. It's raining. Do you _____ want to take a walk?

    a. smart   **b.** still   **c.** career   **d.** throughout

28. With regular practice, you are sure to _____. Good luck!

    a. succeed   **b.** compare   **c.** affect   **d.** explain

See the Answer Key on page 207.

CELEBRATIONS

CHAPTER 17

Songkran

Celebrating the new year in Bangkok

GETTING READY TO READ

Talk about these questions with a partner or in a small group.

1. What do you see in the photo?

2. Do you celebrate the start of a new year? When does the new year begin? What do you do?

3. What other new year celebrations do you know about? Make a list.

READING

Look at the words and pictures next to the reading. Then read without stopping. Don't worry about new words. Don't stop to use a dictionary. Just keep reading!

Songkran

1   In many places, a new year begins on January 1.[1] Not everywhere, however. New year celebrations **take place** at other times, too. The date when a new year starts depends on the country, the **culture**, or the **religion**. There are also different ways to celebrate. People may clean house, **put on** new clothes, eat special foods, or throw a party.[2] In Thailand, people celebrate the new year in April, and they do it with water.

2   The month of April is **extremely** hot in Thailand. That may be one reason why water is important in the new year celebration there. Water helps people feel cool, clean, and **fresh**, and a new year is a time for a fresh start.[3]

3   The Thai name for the new year **holiday** is *Songkran*. The celebration begins in the middle of April and **lasts** for several days. Thais look forward to it for a variety of reasons.

4   Children get ready by collecting things like buckets.[4] They will celebrate Songkran by **pouring** water on each other, throwing water at each other, and **shooting** at each other with water guns. They sometimes get adults wet, too. If you want to stay dry, you **had better** stay inside.

5   Jad Kanchanalak grew up in Thailand. She remembers all the fun of Songkran. Jad says, "We always played outside in front of our house in Bangkok. I **used to** get wet and stay wet all day! Nobody really minded getting wet. Everyone **expected** it. It was part of the holiday fun."

6   Older people look forward to the more serious traditions of Songkran. For example, many Thais make visits to temples[5] during the holiday. This is also a time for families to be

(continued)

[1] *January 1* = read "January first"

[2] *throw a party* = plan and have a party

[3] *a fresh start* = a new beginning

[4] *a bucket*

[5] a Buddhist *temple*

together. It is **traditional** for people to go see their older relatives. They visit them to show their respect. Everyone **wishes** each other good luck in the coming year.

7   Jad remembers, "We used to make one or two visits to relatives. Then my sisters and I were free to play. Songkran is a very happy time."

Quick Comprehension Check

Read these sentences about the reading. Circle T (true) or F (false).

1. Everyone around the world celebrates the new year on the same day.   T   F

2. People in Thailand celebrate Songkran in April.   T   F

3. The weather in Thailand is cool in April.   T   F

4. Thai children celebrate the new year by throwing water at people.   T   F

5. Songkran has some serious traditions, too.   T   F

6. It is a time for families to be together.   T   F

EXPLORING VOCABULARY

Thinking about the Target Vocabulary

 Find the words and phrases in bold in "Songkran" on pages 165 and 166. Write them in the list in alphabetical order.

1. culture	6.	11.
2. expected	7.	12.
3.	8.	13.
4.	9.	14.
5.	10.	15.

B Which words and phrases are new to you? Circle them here. Then find them in the reading. Look at the context. Can you guess the meaning?

Using the Target Vocabulary

 **A** Label these pictures. Write *extremely*, *pouring*, *putting on*, or *shooting*.

1. She's _____ a water gun.

2. He's _____ coffee.

3. She's _____ her shoes.

4. The man on the right is _____ tall.

These sentences are about the reading. Complete them with the words and phrases in the box.

cultures	fresh	holiday	religion	traditional	wishing
expect	had better	lasts	take place	used to	

1. Many new year celebrations _____ on January 1 and the night before. That is when they happen.

2. New year celebrations are not the same in all _____. This word means groups with their own traditions, beliefs, art, music, and so on.

3. A _____ is a set of beliefs that a group of people hold. These beliefs are about life and a god or gods.

4. When you are hot, dirty, or tired, water helps you feel cool, clean, and _____.

5. Songkran is a _____, so schools and most businesses are closed.

6. Songkran doesn't end after just one day. This holiday _____ for several days.

7. If you don't want to get wet during Songkran, here is some strong advice: You _____ not go outside.

8. Jad always loved Songkran. It was always hot, and she _____ stay wet all day.

9. Jad says that everyone knows that they will get wet. They _____ to get wet.

10. On holidays, people often do the same things every year. They do the things that are _____ in their culture.

11. When you tell people "Happy New Year!" you are _____ them a happy year. You are telling them you hope it will be a good year for them.

These sentences use the target words and phrases **in new contexts.**
Complete them with the words and phrases in the box.

culture	fresh	holiday	religions	traditional	wish
expect	had better	last	take place	used to	

1. It's good for your health to eat a lot of _____ fruit and vegetables.

2. Buddhism, Islam, and Christianity are _____.

3. I _____ trust him, but I don't trust him anymore.

4. They called me before my test to _____ me luck.

5. Those fresh-cut flowers are beautiful, but they won't _____ long.

6. Slava thought he would get to class on time. He didn't _____ to be late.

7. Jiselle is in Moscow. She's learning about Russian _____: how the people of Russia think and act, what they believe, and so on.

8. The Fourth of July, Independence Day, is an important _____ in the United States.

9. In some cultures, it is _____ to wear black when a relative has died.

10. He _____ tell the truth. He'll get into trouble if he doesn't.

11. When and where did the meeting _____?

Word Grammar: *Used To*

In Unit 3, you practiced *be used to* + noun/pronoun. When you are used to something, it isn't new or strange for you. For example:

*The nurse didn't mind the sight of blood. She **was used to** it.*

*I'm working nights now, and it's hard. I'**m not used to** this schedule.*

Used to + the base form of a verb has a different meaning. It shows that an action happened regularly in the past but doesn't happen now. For example:

*He **used to smoke**. (He stopped smoking. He doesn't smoke anymore.)*

*She **used to have** a Toyota. Then she sold it. Now she has a Honda.*

Write these sentences in a different way. Use *used to* + a verb or *be used to* (something).

1. She stopped going to that school. *She used to go to that school.*

2. I always watch American movies. *I'm used to watching American movies.*

3. He stopped working part-time. _____

   _____

4. We always have hot weather. _____

   _____

5. I always work on one type of computer. _____

   _____

   _____

6. You stopped giving me advice. _____

   _____

DEVELOPING YOUR SKILLS

Reading for Details

Are these statements about "Songkran" true or false? If the reading doesn't give the information, check (✓) "It doesn't say."

	True	False	It doesn't say.
1. *Songkran* is the name for the Thai new year celebration.	✓		
2. Songkran begins on January 1 in Thailand.			
3. The weather in Thailand is always hot.			
4. Songkran lasts for several weeks.			
5. Thai children look forward to this holiday.			
6. Jad used to play outside and stay wet all day.			
7. It is traditional to visit relatives at Songkran.			
8. Songkran is Thailand's most important holiday.			

Summarizing

Use information from the reading to complete this summary.

People in _____ (1) celebrate the start of

_____ (2) in April. The name of the celebration is

_____ (3). They celebrate the holiday with _____ (4).

Children _____ (5). Families visit

_____ (6) and _____ (7) during Songkran.

Interviewing

Read the questions in the chart. Write your answers. Then interview a partner. Write your partner's answers.

	You	Your Partner
1. What was your favorite holiday when you were a child?		
2. What did you use to do on this holiday?		
3. What holidays do you celebrate now?		
4. Would you like to visit Thailand during Songkran?		

Using New Words

These questions use some of the target words. Ask and answer the questions with a partner. Then talk about your answers with the class.

1. Name a **fresh** fruit that tastes good.
2. Name three **religions**.
3. Tell when you **wish** someone good luck.
4. Tell something you **had better** do or you will get in trouble.
5. Tell something you **expect** to do, and tell when you expect to do it.

Writing

Write about a holiday that you used to enjoy as a child. Describe your holiday traditions. What did you use to do? You can begin: *When I was a child, my favorite holiday was _____. (I / My family) used to . . .*

CHAPTER 18

Québec's Winter Carnival

Inside the Ice Hotel

GETTING READY TO READ

Talk about these questions with a partner or in a small group.

1. Which is more of a problem for you, being too hot or being too cold? Why?

2. In cold weather, do you like to be inside or outside? What do you enjoy doing in cold weather?

3. Can you label these pictures of winter sports? Write *skiing*, *skating*, or *dogsled racing* under each picture.

a. _____   b. _____   c. _____

173

READING

Look at the words and pictures next to the reading. Then read without stopping.

Québec's Winter Carnival

1   Winters in the city of Québec, Canada, are very cold. There is snow and ice all around. The days are short, and the nights are long. It does not **sound** like much fun, does it? But the city is beautiful in the snow. For the people of Québec, it is the **perfect** time to celebrate. They do that with a big party that starts in late January and lasts for three weeks. It is the Québec Winter Carnival, and it is the largest winter **festival** in the world.

2   There are many things to do in the city at Carnival. You can walk around and see the fine stone buildings and the beautiful churches. You can watch dogsled races through the **narrow** streets. There are also canoe[1] races on the **wide** Saint Lawrence River. If you get cold, choose one of Québec's great restaurants and have a good, hot meal.

[1] *a canoe*

3   Outside the city, you can go skiing or skating, or you can try to climb a wall of ice. You can even drive a dogsled yourself. At night, you will **be able to** watch fireworks.[2] Then **afterwards**, you can go to sleep in a hotel made of ice!

[2] *fireworks*

4   Yes, it is true. Outside the city, there is a hotel completely made of ice and snow. The Ice Hotel opens for business in January. It stays open for about three months. Its walls of ice are several feet **thick**. There is a bar inside the hotel with tables and chairs made of ice. Ten-year-old Bobby visited the bar with his father, and they **ordered** a **couple** of sodas.[3] Their drinks came in glasses made of ice. **While** he was there, Bobby used a computer in the bar to e-mail his friends and relatives. He sent them photos of himself at the Ice Hotel.

[3] *a soda* = a soft drink, such as Coke or Pepsi

5   Perhaps you are wondering about the beds in this hotel. The beds are all made of ice, too. They have deerskins[4] on top. The rooms are only about 25°F (–5°C), so the hotel gives each

[4] *Deerskins* come from deer.

guest a warm sleeping bag.[5] Bobby and his father had to wear their hats to bed, too.

[5] a *sleeping bag*

6   Maybe you would like the chance to stay at the Ice Hotel. Does it sound like an interesting **experience**? Hundreds of guests stay there each year, but almost no one stays a second night. Maybe you **would rather** stay at a **regular** hotel, with a fine restaurant and nice, warm beds. Either way,[6] beautiful Québec has something for everyone during Carnival.

[6] *either way* = it doesn't matter which one

Quick Comprehension Check

Read these sentences about the reading. Circle T (true) or F (false).

1. Winters are very cold in Québec, Canada.   T F

2. Québec's Winter Carnival lasts for three months. T F

3. There are many things to do in and around the city. T F

4. People can stay at a hotel made of ice.   T F

5. The hotel has just the usual type of beds.   T F

6. Québec is a beautiful city.   T F

EXPLORING VOCABULARY

Thinking about the Target Vocabulary

 A **Find the words and phrases in bold in "Quebec's Winter Carnival" on pages 174 and 175. Write them in the list in alphabetical order.**

1. afterwards	6.	11.
2. be able to	7.	12.
3.	8.	13.
4.	9.	14.
5.	10.	15.

Which words and phrases are new to you? Circle them in the list on page 175. Then find the words and phrases in the reading. Look at the context. Can you guess the meaning?

Using the Target Vocabulary

A These sentences are **about the reading**. What is the meaning of each **boldfaced** word or phrase? Circle a, b, or c.

1. Winter Carnival in Québec is the world's largest winter **festival**. *Festival* means
   a. a celebration.   **b.** a type of sport.   **c.** a time of bad weather.

2. The streets of Québec are **narrow**, so they can be a problem for buses and big trucks. *Narrow* means
   a. nice and clean.   **b.** very old.   **c.** not big across.

3. People at Carnival **are able to** see fireworks at night. *Are able to* means
   a. can.   **b.** have to.   **c.** never.

4. You can watch the fireworks and then go to the Ice Hotel **afterwards**. *Afterwards* means
   a. instead.   **b.** later.   **c.** throughout.

5. Bobby and his father **ordered** drinks in the hotel bar. In this sentence, *ordered* means
   a. put on.   **b.** asked a waiter for.   **c.** argued about.

6. They got a **couple** of sodas. *A couple of something* means
   a. two.   **b.** ten.   **c.** many.

7. The Ice Hotel has warm sleeping bags for its **guests**. The guests are its
   a. prisoners.   **b.** patients.   **c.** visitors.

8. Most hotels aren't made of ice, but the Ice Hotel isn't a **regular** hotel. In this sentence, *regular* means
   a. of the usual kind.   **b.** secret.   **c.** dangerous.

9. Some people would like to stay at the Ice Hotel. Others **would rather** stay at another hotel. *Would rather* means
   a. would hate to.   **b.** would like it better to.   **c.** would never.

B These sentences use the target words and phrases **in new contexts.**
Complete them with the words and phrases in the box.

afterwards	couple	festival	narrow	regular
be able to	'd rather	guests	order	

1. These shoes hurt my feet. They're too _____.

2. Each student can bring four people to graduation. That's right—only four _____ per student.

3. There is a famous film _____ at Cannes in France. People go there to see many new movies.

4. He can't fail any more courses. If he fails another, he won't _____ graduate.

5. This restaurant has a great variety of good food. It's hard to decide what to _____!

6. First, let's get all the facts. Then _____, we can make a decision.

7. I'm sorry to keep you waiting. I'll be ready in a _____ of minutes.

8. Let's not go out to the movies. I _____ stay home and watch a movie here.

9. He is too tall to buy clothes in a _____ store. He has to order specially made clothes.

C Read these sentences. Match the **boldfaced** target words with their definitions.

a. You should be a lawyer. That's the **perfect** profession for you.

b. We saw some unusual birds **while** we were walking on the beach.

c. I didn't like my job in the factory. Working there wasn't a good **experience**.

d. Tell me more about your project. It **sounds** interesting.

e. The building has **thick** walls, so it's quiet inside.

f. It's a **wide** lake. It's more than 100 miles across.

Target Words	Definitions
1. _____	= large across, not narrow (*a . . . street, a . . . river*)
2. _____	= large between its two sides, not thin (*. . . ice, . . . books*)
3. _____	= exactly right, the best
4. _____	= during the time that
5. _____	= something that happens to a person
6. _____	= seems (because of information you heard or read)

Word Grammar: Measure Words + Adjectives

Adjectives such as *thick*, *wide*, and *tall* can follow measure words
(such as *feet* or *miles*) to tell how big something or someone is:
   The river is about a mile **wide**.
   He is six feet, two inches **tall**.
   Our apartment building is six stories **high**.

Write your answers to these questions. Use a number + a measure word + *thick/wide/tall/long/high*.

1. How thick is your fattest book? It's about 2 inches thick. _____

   _____

2. How high is the building you live in? _____

   _____

3. How tall are you? _____

   _____

4. How long is your hair? _____

   _____

5. How wide is the room you are in? _____

   _____

DEVELOPING YOUR SKILLS

Topics of Paragraphs

A Look at the list of paragraph topics from "Québec's Winter Carnival." Find the paragraph on each topic in the reading. Write the paragraph number (1–6).

a. the Ice Hotel   Paragraph ____

b. winter and the festival in Québec   Paragraph ____

c. choosing a hotel   Paragraph ____

d. things to do in the city during Carnival   Paragraph ____

e. things to do outside the city   Paragraph ____

f. beds in the Ice Hotel   Paragraph ____

B Write a sentence about each topic from Part A. Use information from the reading.

1. _____

2. _____

3. _____

4. _____

5. _____

6. _____

The Main Idea

Complete the following statement to tell the main idea of the reading.

There are many interesting things to do at Québec's Winter Carnival,

such as _____

_____.

Discussion

Talk about these questions with a partner or in a small group. Then share your answers with the class.

1. Would you like to go to Québec in the winter, or would you rather go somewhere warm? Why?

2. Would you like to be a guest at the Ice Hotel? Why or why not?

3. Would you rather go skiing or dogsled racing? Or would you rather do neither one? Why?

4. What other festivals do you know about?

Using New Words

Work alone or with a partner. Choose five target words or phrases from the list on page 175. On a piece of paper, use each word or phrase in a sentence.

Writing

Imagine the perfect restaurant meal. Answer the questions. Then write a paragraph.

1. Where would you eat?
   The perfect meal for me would be in/at _____.

2. Who would be with you?
   _____ would be my guest/guests.

3. What would you eat?
   First we would eat _____. Then, we would have

   _____.

4. What would you drink?
   We would drink _____.

5. What kind of music would you listen to?
   While we were eating, we would listen to _____.

6. What would you do afterwards?
   After the meal, I would _____.

Example:

   The perfect meal for me would be in a great restaurant at the top of
   a tall building at night. My girlfriend would be my guest. . . .

CHAPTER 19

Celebrating a New Baby

A proud father with his new baby

GETTING READY TO READ

Talk about these questions with a partner or in a small group.

1. What do you see in the photo?

2. Have you ever celebrated the birth of a new baby? Who was the baby? What did you do to celebrate?

3. Who gave you your name? Why did they choose it? Does your name have a special meaning?

181

READING

Look at the words and picture next to the reading. Then read without stopping.

Celebrating a New Baby

1   What did your parents do to celebrate when you were born? Of course, you cannot remember, but maybe they have photos from a ceremony[1] of some kind. People usually have ceremonies to mark important **events**. **Weddings** are a perfect example. Getting married is an important event, and **so** is having a baby. In most cultures, there are traditional ceremonies and other ways to celebrate a new child.

2   When a baby is born, it is an **exciting** time for the parents. They usually want to tell their neighbors the good news. Proud parents in the United States often do this by decorating[2] their front door with balloons.[3] Pink balloons mean the baby is a girl. Blue ones are for boys. **Gifts** of baby clothes are often pink or blue, too.

3   In most parts of the world, there are **religious** or **cultural** ceremonies for new babies. In Mexico, many parents **dress up** their babies and take them to church. In some African cultures, the family **plants** a tree. Ceremonies often take place when babies are a particular[4] number of days old. In China and Korea, this happens on the baby's 100th day.

4   New babies everywhere **have one thing in common**: they all need names. Some parents choose a name before the child is born. Others wait **until** afterwards. Parents in some cultures think it is unlucky, even dangerous, to choose a name too soon. For their own **protection**, Chinese babies may get just a "milk name" at first. They may not get their real name until they are a month old or more.

5   Choosing a baby's name is not always left up to[5] the parents. Sometimes the name depends on cultural traditions.

---

[1] a *ceremony* = a formal group of actions and words used at a religious or public event

[2] *decorate* = make a thing or a place look nicer by adding things to it

[3] *balloons*

[4] *particular* = this one and not any other

[5] *left up to* = to be decided by

Here are the **rules** for naming a baby in Somalia:
- The first name is up to the parents.
- The middle name is the first name of the father.
- The last name is the first name of the father's father.

So Nasra Suleiman Ali is actually "Nasra, daughter of Suleiman, granddaughter of Ali."

6   It is **common** for parents of new babies to receive gifts, such as baby clothes, flowers, or money. Gifts, money, celebrations—all these things are **wonderful**. But what do most new parents really need? More sleep!

Quick Comprehension Check

Read these sentences about the reading. Circle *T* (true) or *F* (false).

1. People mark important times in their lives with celebrations.   T   F

2. U.S. parents usually want to keep news of a new baby private.   T   F

3. New parents in the United States usually decorate their cars.   T   F

4. New baby celebrations often depend on the family's religion or culture.   T   F

5. Ceremonies for new babies last 100 days.   T   F

6. In Somalia, there are cultural traditions for naming a baby.   T   F

EXPLORING VOCABULARY

Thinking about the Target Vocabulary

 A Find the words and phrases in **bold** in "Celebrating a New Baby" on pages 182 and 183. Write them in the list in alphabetical order.

1. common	6.	11.
2. cultural	7.	12.
3.	8.	13.
4.	9.	14.
5.	10.	15.

 B Which words and phrases are new to you? Circle them here. Then find them in the reading. Look at the context. Can you guess the meaning?

Using the Target Vocabulary

 A These sentences are **about the reading**. Complete them with the words and phrases in the box.

dressing up	have one thing	protection	rules	until
exciting	in common	religious	so	wonderful

1. Getting married is an important thing to do, and _____ is having a baby. Having a baby is important, too.
2. Having a baby is an _____ event. It makes people happy and interested in what is happening.
3. Some people have a _____ ceremony for a new baby, maybe in a church or temple.
4. "_____" means putting on your best clothes, usually for an important event, or putting special clothes on someone else, such as a baby.

5. All new babies _____: They need names. This is true for all new babies.

6. Some parents name a child before he or she is born. Some parents wait _____ later, after the baby is born.

7. When you do something to keep a baby safe, you do it for the baby's _____.

8. Parents in Somalia follow _____ for naming a baby. These tell parents what they have to do.

9. Gifts, money, and celebrations are all great things. They're _____.

B These sentences use the target words and phrases **in new contexts.** Complete them with the words and phrases in the box.

dress up	have nothing	protection	rules	until
exciting	in common	religious	so	wonderful

1. We had a _____ day at the beach—lots of fun, and very relaxing.

2. Would you like to travel around the world? It would be an _____ experience!

3. She's going to be twenty-two and _____ am I.

4. They can't play the game if they don't follow the _____.

5. She loves to _____, but he'd rather wear the same old clothes all the time.

6. He usually goes to bed at 10:00 P.M., but last night he stayed up _____ midnight.

7. The whole family belongs to the same church. They have the same _____ beliefs.

8. Please put on your seat belt in the car. It's there for your _____.

9. I don't know what to talk to him about. We _____.

Read these sentences. Match the boldfaced target words with their definitions.

a. Carmen and her husband have the same last name, Garcia. It's a very **common** name.

b. Ann and David's **wedding** will take place in a church in her hometown.

c. In the spring, I **plant** flowers and vegetables in my garden.

d. People can learn about world **events** by reading the newspaper, watching TV, or going online.

e. Is Christmas Day a religious holiday, or a **cultural** event, or both?

f. We always give our mother a **gift** on her birthday.

Target Words	Definitions
1. _____	= usual; easy to find because there are many
2. _____	= put (something) into the ground so it can grow
3. _____	= things that happen, especially important or unusual things
4. _____	= a present, something that you give to someone you like
5. _____	= relating to a group of people and their way of life
6. _____	= a ceremony when two people get married

Word Grammar: Count and Noncount Nouns

There are **count nouns** and **noncount nouns** in English.

Notes	Examples
• Count nouns have a singular form and a plural form.	one **book**, two **books** one **man**, several **men**
• Noncount nouns have only one form.	The **air** is cool.
• Don't use a, an, or a number before a noncount noun.	She gave me a̷ good advice.
• Don't add -(e)s.	Do we have homework̷s̷?

A Complete the chart. Write each noncount noun in the right category.

advice   fun   information   milk   protection
blood   gold   juice   music   tea
education   history   land   paper   time
exercise   ice   love   plastic   water

Liquids	
Solids	
Ideas, things you can't touch	

B Write sentences with noncount nouns from Part A.

1. _Milk is good for your bones._
2. _____
3. _____
4. _____
5. _____

DEVELOPING YOUR SKILLS

Reading for Details

Are these statements about "Celebrating a New Baby" true or false? If the reading doesn't give the information, check (✓) "It doesn't say."

	True	False	It doesn't say.
1. People have ceremonies to mark big events in their lives.			
2. In the United States, pink is for baby girls, and blue is for baby boys.			
3. In Mexico, the family plants a tree when a baby is born.			
4. In Korea, parents wait ten days to celebrate.			
5. Some Chinese babies get "milk names."			
6. In many cultures, the grandparents decide on the child's name.			
7. People often give gifts to new parents.			

Sentences with *Because*

A   Complete the sentences. Use information from the reading.

1. Some U.S. parents decorate their front door because _____

_____ .

2. Some African parents plant a tree because _____

_____ .

3. Some Chinese parents wait to give their babies names because _____

_____ .

4. Nasra has her father's and grandfather's names because _____

_____ .

B   Complete this sentence. Then compare answers with a partner.

I (like / don't like) my name because _____

_____ .

Summarizing

Write answers to these questions on a piece of paper. Then use your answers to write a summary of the reading. Write your summary as a paragraph.

1. Why do people celebrate a new baby?
2. What do people around the world often do to celebrate?
3. What kinds of ceremonies are there?
4. What is an example of an American tradition?
5. What do babies in every culture need?
6. How do some babies get their names?

Discussion

Talk about these questions in a small group or with the whole class.

1. Why do you think Koreans wait 100 days to celebrate a new baby?
2. Why do you think some Africans plant a tree when a baby is born?
3. Why do you think some people say it's bad to name a child too soon?
4. If your parents followed the Somali tradition for naming a baby, what would your name be?

Using New Words

Work with a partner. Choose five target words or phrases from the list on page 184. On a piece of paper, use each word or phrase in a sentence.

Writing

A Timeline

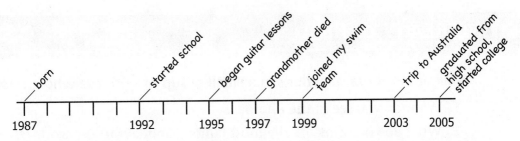

Draw a timeline of your life. Mark the important events in your life, from the day you were born to the present. Then write a paragraph about your life. You can begin:

I was born in _____. **You can introduce sentences like this:** At age _____, I . . . or In 19____ / 20____, I . . .

CHAPTER 20

Some Unusual Celebrations

Celebrating La Tomatina

GETTING READY TO READ

Talk about these questions in a small group or with the whole class.

1. What do you see in the photo?
2. What do you think are the most famous holidays in the world?
3. What special days are celebrated in your country that people from other countries probably don't know about?

READING

Look at the words and pictures next to the reading. Then read without stopping.

Some Unusual Celebrations

1   Some holidays are well-known all around the world. Among them are New Year's Eve celebrations. Also common are days in honor of[1] love and **friendship**, like Valentine's Day. Each country has its own special holidays, too, often to mark important events in its history. Schools, banks, and government offices all close on days like these. Some of the days people celebrate, however, are **less** serious. A few of them are really very strange.

[1] *in honor of* = to celebrate

2   Of course, they are not strange to the people who celebrate them. Perhaps that is because the celebrations have long traditions. Consider April Fool's Day, for example. No one knows when or why it began. Today it is celebrated in many countries—France, England, and Australia, among others. On this day, people play practical jokes.[2] Jokes **are supposed to** be **funny**, but these jokes do not make everyone laugh. The ones who laugh are the ones playing the jokes. The people they fool[3] often get angry. Does celebrating this day **make sense** to you?

[2] *play practical jokes* = trick someone so that others laugh at him or her

[3] *fool* = make someone believe something that is not true

3   Dyngus Day in Poland seems strange, too. On this day, it is traditional for boys to pour water over the heads of girls. Here is the strangest part: They do it to girls they like.

4   Other unusual celebrations take place in a **single** city or town. A holiday called *La Tomatina* is celebrated in Buñol, Spain. Every year, in late August, big trucks carry more than 200,000 **pounds** of tomatoes into this little town. Then begins the world's biggest food fight. For two hours, people in the streets throw tomatoes at each other. Everyone **ends up** red from head to **toe**.

5   August 10 marks the start of the Puck Fair, an Irish festival with a very unusual tradition. People from the town of Killorglin go up into the mountains and catch a **wild** goat.[4]

[4] *a mountain goat*

(continued)

They bring him back to town, put a crown[5] on his head, and make him king for three days.

[5] a *crown*

6   There are also some celebrations that are really **weird**. In the United States, sometimes one person gets an idea for a new holiday and tries to get others to accept it. Whose idea was **Public** Sleeping Day? That one is on February 28. It may seem strange, but it sounds like more fun than the one on February 9. That is supposed to be Toothache[6] Day.

[6] a *toothache* = a tooth that hurts

7   Do you like the idea of **inventing** a new holiday? If you do, then you will want to mark March 26 on your **calendar**. That is **Make Up** Your Own Holiday Day.

Quick Comprehension Check

Read these sentences about the reading. Circle T (true) or F (false).

1. New year celebrations are common around the world.   T   F

2. Valentine's Day is an example of an unusual celebration.   T   F

3. Small towns sometimes have their own holidays.   T   F

4. On the day called La Tomatina, people throw baseballs at each other.   T   F

5. Some people have fun imagining new holidays.   T   F

EXPLORING VOCABULARY

Thinking about the Target Vocabulary

 Find the words and phrases in bold in "Some Unusual Celebrations" on pages 191 and 192. Write them in the list in alphabetical order.

1. are supposed to   6.   11.

2. calendar   7.   12.

3.   8.   13.

4.   9.   14.

5.   10.   15.

B Which words and phrases are new to you? Circle them in the list on page 192. Then find them in the reading. Look at the context. Can you guess the meaning?

Using the Target Vocabulary

 A Complete the sentences about the pictures. Write *calendar*, *pounds*, *public*, or *toes*.

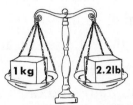

1. A kilo, or kilogram, equals 2.2 _____ .

2. She's marking her _____ .

3. He's sleeping in a _____ park.

4. You have fingers on your hands and _____ on your feet.

 B These sentences are **about the reading**. Complete them with the words and phrases in the box.

ends up	funny	is supposed to	make sense	single	wild
friendship	invents	less		make up	weird

1. Valentine's Day is a celebration of both love and _____ , the relationship between two friends.

2. There are important reasons for some holidays, such as remembering people who died in wars. Other holidays are _____ serious. They are not as serious.

3. A joke _____ make people laugh. That is what we expect of a joke.

4. Stories, jokes, and movies that are _____ make people smile or laugh.

5. There are good reasons for many holidays. They are easy to understand. But some celebrations do not _____. It is hard to explain them.

6. Some holidays are widely known. Others are celebrated in a _____ place (just one city, town, or country).

7. When someone _____ in a situation, it often means that he or she arrived in that situation without planning it.

8. For the Puck Fair, people go up into the mountains and catch a _____ goat. This kind of goat runs free, unlike the ones that live on farms.

9. Some days we celebrate are just a little strange. Others are really _____.

10. The person who _____ a holiday is the first person to think of it. Use this verb to describe making new machines or figuring out new ways to do things.

11. March 26 is a day to _____, or imagine, new holidays. This verb can also be used with *a story* or *a song*. Use this verb with *a reason* or *an explanation* when you mean that the reason or explanation is not true.

C These sentences use the target words and phrases **in new contexts.** Complete them with the words and phrases in the box.

are supposed to	friendship	invented	make sense	single	wild
ended up	funny	less	make up	weird	

1. All players _____ follow the rules of the game.

2. We wanted to go to Penn Station, but we took the wrong train, and we _____ at Grand Central Station.

3. They had a lot in common, and their _____ grew quickly.

4. You can buy a ticket for a _____ bus ride, or you can buy a ticket good for ten rides.

5. There are _____ horses running free in Mongolia.

6. No one believed her explanation because it didn't _____.

7. He was so _____ that I laughed until I cried.

8. James Naismith _____ the game of basketball in 1891.

9. I don't have a good reason for being late, so I'll _____ something.

10. Some of his ideas sound good, but a few sound _____ or even crazy.

11. The first movie was really exciting. The second was _____ exciting but still good.

Word Grammar: Quantifiers with Noncount Nouns

Quantifiers are words that tell how many or how much.
- Use the following quantifiers with noncount nouns:
  much, a lot of, enough, some, any, a little, and *no.*
  We need *a **little*** sugar for our tea.
- Use *any* and *much* only with negative verbs or in questions.
  We don't have ***much*** time. Is there ***any*** snow?
- Don't use a negative verb with the quantifier *no.*
  They ~~don't~~ have no money.

Write sentences with a quantifier + noncount noun. Choose from these nouns: *advice, exercise, fun, gold, ice, luck, news, plastic, research, respect, responsibility,* **and** *success.*

1. A lot of gold comes from South Africa. _____

2. _____

3. _____

4. _____

5. _____

6. _____

DEVELOPING YOUR SKILLS

Reading for Details

Are these statements about "Some Unusual Celebrations" true or false? If the reading doesn't give the information, check (✓) "It doesn't say."

	True	False	It doesn't say.
1. Many cultures have special days to celebrate love and friendship.			
2. Some days that people celebrate are unusual and strange.			
3. Schools are closed on important holidays.			
4. Everyone enjoys April Fool's Day.			
5. April Fool's Day is celebrated in the United States and Canada.			
6. Girls in Poland think Dyngus Day is fun.			
7. The tomato fight in Buñol, Spain, lasts two hours.			
8. The Puck Fair is held in Killorglin, Ireland.			
9. Public Sleeping Day is a traditional U.S. holiday.			
10. March 26 is a day to invent new holidays.			

Summarizing

 Use information from the reading to complete these sentences.

1. Some special days celebrate important ideas, like love and

   _____.

2. Others celebrate important events in a country's _____.

3. However, some special days are less _____, and some are really _____.

4. One unusual celebration is _____.

5. Other strange holidays take place in a single _____, such as _____ in _____.

6. There are also some weird holidays, like _____.

On a piece of paper, write your sentences in paragraph form to make a summary of the reading.

Discussion

Talk in a small group or with the whole class.

1. Name three of the celebrations described in the reading. Tell what you know about each one.

2. Which of the celebrations described in the reading is the strangest? Why do you think so?

3. If you could make up a new holiday, what would it be? Who or what would you celebrate, and how?

Using New Words

Work with a partner. Choose five target words or phrases from the list on page 192. On a piece of paper, use each word or phrase in a sentence.

Writing

Choose one of these topics and write a paragraph.

1. Write about something you celebrated with friends. What was the reason for the celebration? What did you do to celebrate?

2. Describe something funny that happened to you or something you did to make others laugh.

3. Describe how you celebrated the start of this year or how you plan to celebrate the next new year.

UNIT 5 Wrap-up

REVIEWING VOCABULARY

A What part of speech are the words in each group? Cross out the one that does not belong. Check (✓) *Nouns*, *Verbs*, or *Adjectives*.

				Nouns	Verbs	Adjectives
1. event	calendar	~~traditional~~	toe	✓	☐	☐
2. public	wild	weird	gift	☐	☐	☐
3. couple	pour	invent	expect	☐	☐	☐
4. religion	last	protection	friendship	☐	☐	☐
5. rule	regular	common	perfect	☐	☐	☐
6. religious	cultural	exciting	festival	☐	☐	☐

B Complete these sentences with the phrases in the box. There are two extra phrases.

be able to	had better	supposed to	used to
dress up	make sense	take place	would rather
end up	put on	have something in common	

1. We invited them to our wedding, but they won't _____ come.
2. When will the event _____?
3. We _____. We both like to dance.
4. Everyone is _____ tell the truth in court.
5. I don't want to eat pizza again! I _____ get something else.
6. He _____ be a student here, but he graduated.

198

7. I read the story twice, but it still didn't _____ to me.

8. If your feet are cold, _____ some shoes.

9. You had better pay the bill now or you'll _____ having to pay more later.

EXPANDNG VOCABULARY

Synonyms and Antonyms

Two words with the same meaning are **synonyms**, like *big* and *large*.

Two words with opposite meanings are **antonyms**, like *big* and *little*.

What is the relationship between the following pairs of words? Check (✓) *Synonyms* or *Antonyms*.

	Synonyms	Antonyms
1. thick – thin	☐	☑
2. narrow – wide	☐	☐
3. lasted – continued	☐	☐
4. afterwards – later	☐	☐
5. take place – happen	☐	☐
6. funny – serious	☐	☐
7. less – more	☐	☐
8. guest – visitor	☐	☐
9. make up – invent	☐	☐
10. regular – unusual	☐	☐

A PUZZLE

Complete the sentences with words you studied in Chapters 17–20. Write the words in the puzzle.

Across

1. Thank you! I had a w_____ time.
3. These vegetables are f_____ from the garden.
4. When you travel, you can learn about other c_____.
6. The police officer said he had to s_____ the man.
9. Please wait w_____ I find out.
10. We p_____ flowers every spring.

Down

1. At bedtime, she w_____ the children "sweet dreams."
2. The stores will be open u_____ 9:00 P.M.
5. The dark side of the moon is e_____ cold.
6. Marisol likes to dress up, and s_____ does Rosa.
7. Let's tell the waiter we're ready to o_____.
8. That s_____ like a great idea!

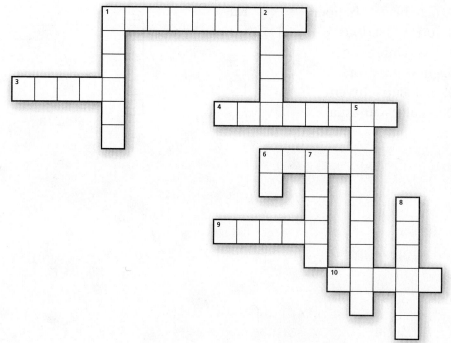

DICTIONARY SKILLS

 A Look at this dictionary entry. Then answer the questions.

> **news** /nuz/ *n* [U] information about something that has just happened: *We watch the news on television.* | *Have you heard any news about Terry?*

- Do you see the symbol [U]? It stands for *uncountable* or *noncount*. *News* is a noncount noun, so it has no plural form. You can say *much* or *a little news*, but not ~~many~~ or ~~two~~ *news*.
- Does your dictionary have a symbol or an abbreviation for noncount nouns?

  ☐ Yes, it has this (symbol/abbreviation): _____
  ☐ No, it doesn't have one.

B Sometimes a noun can be both a noncount and a count noun. Look at this dictionary entry.

> **ex•pe•ri•ence**[1] /ɪkˈspɪriəns/ *n* **1** something that happens to you: *The accident was an experience she will never forget.* **2** [U] knowledge or skill that you get from doing a job: *She is a teacher with 5 years of experience.*

What kind of noun is *experience* in these sentences? Check (✔) *Count* or *Noncount*.

Count   Noncount

✔   _____ 1. Our visit to Québec was a wonderful experience.

_____ _____ 2. Do you have much experience with computers?

_____ _____ 3. Doctors have experience with medical emergencies.

_____ _____ 4. Tell us about your experiences at the festival.

C Write one sentence with *experience* as a count noun and one with *experience* as a noncount noun.

1. _____

2. _____

Vocabulary Self-Test 3

Circle the letter of the word or phrase that best completes each sentence.

Example: The sun goes down in the _____.

      a. artist   **b.** race   **(c.)** west   **d.** result

1. The way that parents take care of a child depends in part on their

   _____.

     a. toes   **b.** culture   **c.** idiom   **d.** shoulder

2. He had a long _____ as a judge.

     a. career   **b.** elbow   **c.** gift   **d.** style

3. The sun shining in _____ the windows made the car very warm.

     a. until   **b.** once   **c.** so   **d.** through

4. What _____ bag can you take on the plane?

     a. pound   **b.** skill   **c.** size   **d.** roof

5. I went with her because she didn't want to go _____.

     a. alone   **b.** smart   **c.** wide   **d.** fresh

6. We waited in the emergency room _____ the doctors took care of him.

     a. along   **b.** actually   **c.** while   **d.** throughout

7. The festival _____ in April.

     a. makes up   **b.** takes place   **c.** dresses up   **d.** can't stand

8. They know each other because they _____ the same club.

     a. plant   **b.** doubt   **c.** pour   **d.** belong to

9. Do you _____ listen to the news on the radio?

     a. ever   **b.** extremely   **c.** either   **d.** else

10. A baby started crying in the _____ of the wedding.

      a. couple   **b.** middle   **c.** experience   **d.** capital

11. He didn't tell anyone the _____ story.

      a. public   **b.** thick   **c.** shy   **d.** whole

12. They quickly _____ friends.

    a. lasted   **b.** wished   **c.** depended   **d.** became

13. The river is _____ a mile wide, maybe a mile and a half.

    a. finally   **b.** until   **c.** about   **d.** especially

14. There are many _____ planned for the New Year's Eve celebration in Rome.

    a. stones   **b.** distances   **c.** events   **d.** opinions

15. He _____ happy when he talks about their relationship.

    a. sounds   **b.** shoots   **c.** matters   **d.** accepts

16. They eat very big meals on holidays but never on _____ days.

    a. empty   **b.** foreign   **c.** regular   **d.** wild

17. I think they're having a _____ discussion. No one is smiling.

    a. wonderful   **b.** serious   **c.** tiny   **d.** funny

18. We _____ drinks to go with our pizza.

    a. trusted   **b.** ordered   **c.** used to   **d.** put on

19. We looked at the _____ to find the time of the next train.

    a. surprise   **b.** friendship   **c.** festival   **d.** schedule

20. Did she give any _____ why she was so worried?

    a. reason   **b.** protection   **c.** trouble   **d.** prison

21. Even a small computer can _____ a lot of information.

    a. wonder   **b.** taste   **c.** store   **d.** argue

22. They began their research five years _____.

    a. instead   **b.** less   **c.** ago   **d.** above

23. Laws are the _____ that everyone in a state, province, or country must follow.

    a. chances   **b.** brains   **c.** holidays   **d.** rules

24. You had better not _____ his name. Keep it a secret.

    a. shine   **b.** mention   **c.** climb   **d.** mind

25. Do you trust the newspaper to give readers the _____?

    a. grades   **b.** farms   **c.** facts   **d.** continents

26. He won the race _____, first in 2008 and then again in 2009.

    a. twice   **b.** several   **c.** away   **d.** still

27. The lawyer asked us a lot of questions, trying to understand our

_____.

    a. shape   **b.** age   **c.** touch   **d.** situation

28. The kitchen is too _____ for a table.

    a. salty   **b.** narrow   **c.** proud   **d.** perfect

29. The British spelling is *travelled*, but in American English, there is a

_____ *l*, not two.

    a. human   **b.** basic   **c.** single   **d.** weird

30. We _____ rain, but the weather was fine.

    a. expected   **b.** counted   **c.** ended up   **d.** were supposed to

31. During the festival, the streets are filled with _____ of foreign

visitors.

    a. courts   **b.** crowds   **c.** calendars   **d.** factories

32. They won't _____ travel because they're in poor health.

    a. be able to   **b.** make sense   **c.** grow up   **d.** go on

33. We expect about 100 _____ at the wedding, most of them

relatives.

    a. guests   **b.** news   **c.** projects   **d.** knees

34. It will taste better if you _____ some salt.

    a. fail   **b.** add   **c.** mark   **d.** fix

35. One of Venezuela's most important _____ is oil.

    a. beaches   **b.** artists   **c.** patients   **d.** products

36. That student never gets a grade _____ 90 percent.

    a. among   **b.** enough   **c.** below   **d.** perhaps

37. I didn't buy it because it wasn't _____ that price.

    a. worth   **b.** special   **c.** best   **d.** usual

38. The scientist wanted to know if a change in temperature would

_____ the results.

    a. give up   **b.** affect   **c.** receive   **d.** describe

39. It's only nine o'clock, but she's _____ in bed for the night.

    a. enough   **b.** too much   **c.** afterwards   **d.** already

40. It was always her _____ to have a career as a singer.

    a. variety   **b.** relationship   **c.** dream   **d.** gold

See the Answer Key on page 208.

VOCABULARY SELF-TESTS ANSWER KEY

Below are the answers to the Vocabulary Self-Tests. Check your answers, and then review any words you did not remember. You can look up the word in the Index to Target Vocabulary on pages 209 and 210. Then go back to the reading and exercises to find the word. Use your dictionary as needed.

Vocabulary Self-Test 1, Units 1–2 (pages 77–78)

1. b. below
2. a. health
3. b. protect
4. c. However
5. c. dangerous
6. c. respect
7. d. actually
8. b. history
9. a. capital

10. c. while
11. d. looking forward to
12. b. gets
13. b. look up
14. d. exercise
15. a. products
16. a. facts
17. d. best

18. c. belong to
19. a. breathe
20. a. own
21. d. strange
22. a. what about
23. c. about
24. b. well
25. a. even

Vocabulary Self-Test 2, Units 3–4 (pages 159–160)

1. c. through
2. b. figure out
3. d. accident
4. a. used to
5. a. followed
6. c. private
7. a. matter
8. b. mention
9. d. idiom
10. c. take care of

11. b. perhaps
12. b. electricity
13. d. At first
14. d. gold
15. b. was born
16. c. schedule
17. a. finally
18. a. match
19. b. relationship

20. c. serious
21. b. dream
22. d. sense
23. c. midnight
24. a. news
25. d. grades
26. c. marks
27. b. still
28. a. succeed

Vocabulary Self-Test 3, Units 1–5 (pages 204–205)

1. b. culture
2. a. career
3. d. through
4. c. size
5. a. alone
6. c. while
7. b. takes place
8. d. belong to
9. a. ever
10. b. middle
11. d. whole
12. d. became
13. c. about
14. c. events
15. a. sounds
16. c. regular
17. b. serious
18. b. ordered
19. d. schedule
20. a. reason
21. c. store
22. c. ago
23. d. rules
24. b. mention
25. c. facts
26. a. twice
27. d. situation
28. b. narrow
29. c. single
30. a. expected
31. b. crowds
32. a. be able to
33. a. guests
34. b. add
35. d. products
36. c. below
37. a. worth
38. b. affect
39. d. already
40. c. dream

INDEX TO TARGET VOCABULARY